Statement of Service of No. 64...

Unit in which served.	Promotions, Reductions, Casualties, &c.	From—	To—	Remarks.
9th Inf Batt	Private	24/8/14	10/9/14	R.O. etc
	Lance Corporal	10/9/14	27-4-15	from RB67/8
9th Btn.	Sgt	28-4-15		D.O. 154
	Awarded the Distinguished Conduct Medal			BR 42B
	Special mention Despatches General Sir Ian Hamilton (Memo from Div. Hd. Qrs Anzac dated 24.8.15)			

5311.

MILITARY FORCES.
IMPERIAL FORCE.
Enlisted for Service Abroad.

MM

Edward Kenyon

24.8.14

I have examined the above details, and find them correct in every respect.

Person Enlisting before Attestation.

THE
GALLIPOLI
LETTER

A NOTE ON THE COVER PORTRAIT

The person standing in the foreground of this picture is Sergeant John Edward Kenyon, 9th Australian Infantry Battalion. John enlisted in Brisbane on 27 August 1914 but he lived mainly at Kyogle in northern New South Wales. He was born at Southampton, Britain, on 27 July 1880. Both his parents had died by the time he was fourteen; he had no brothers or sisters. It is not known when he came to Australia.

John Kenyon was 34 years of age when he enlisted. He described himself as a 'bush worker' and he was 'practically, if not actually engaged' at the time of his enlistment. For his work on the first morning of the landing on 25 April 1915, John Kenyon was awarded the Distinguished Conduct Medal. He had shown 'conspicuous courage and initiative in returning from the firing line under heavy fire, collecting reinforcements, and assisting in leading a successful bayonet charge'. John Kenyon had been lucky to survive the first day: retreating from Lone Pine in the evening he had stumbled across a party of Turkish soldiers who were either too tired or too disorganised to oppose him and he escaped unhurt.

He was promoted to Sergeant on 28 April 1915. John survived at Gallipoli until 25 August 1915 when he was evacuated, sick. Returning in October, he was taken off sick again in December.

While fighting in France, John was awarded the Military Medal for an aggressive raid in the Fleurbaix sector on the night of 1–2 July 1916. The recommendation for the award noted that Kenyon had 'proved absolutely fearless and set a splendid example of gallantry'.

John Kenyon was killed in the fighting at Pozieres on 23 July 1916 and was buried south of the village, in a grave marked with a cross. The marker did not survive the war, and the location of the grave is now unknown. John Kenyon is remembered on the 9th Battalion's memorial tablet at the Australian National Memorial at Villers-Bretonneux, northern France.

The cover salutes a gallant Australian soldier.

THE GALLIPOLI LETTER

KEITH MURDOCH

with an introduction by Michael McKernan
and a foreword by Jack Thompson AM

Facsimiles of the Gallipoli letter by Keith Murdoch, on pp. 71–98, reproduced by permission of the National Library of Australia.

Letters on pp. 65 and 66, regarding Murdoch's appointment to investigate postal facilities in Cairo and Murdoch's letter of introduction, both written by G.F. Pearce in 1915, are copyright Commonwealth of Australia, reproduced by permission.

First published in 2010

Copyright introduction © Michael McKernan 2010
Copyright preface © Jack Thompson 2010

All rights reserved. No part of this book may be reproduced or transmitted in any form or by any means, electronic or mechanical, including photocopying, recording or by any information storage and retrieval system, without prior permission in writing from the publisher. The Australian *Copyright Act 1968* (the Act) allows a maximum of one chapter or 10 per cent of this book, whichever is the greater, to be photocopied by any educational institution for its educational purposes provided that the educational institution (or body that administers it) has given a remuneration notice to Copyright Agency Limited (CAL) under the Act.

Allen & Unwin
83 Alexander Street
Crows Nest NSW 2065
Australia
Phone: (61 2) 8425 0100
Fax: (61 2) 9906 2218
Email: info@allenandunwin.com
Web: www.allenandunwin.com

Cataloguing-in-Publication details are available
from the National Library of Australia
www.librariesaustralia.nla.gov.au

ISBN 978 1 74737 313 3

Set in 11.5/15.5 pt FCaslon 12 by Bookhouse, Sydney
Printed in Australia by McPherson's Printing Group

10 9 8 7 6 5 4 3 2 1

CONTENTS

List of Illustrations	vii
Preface	xii
Introduction	1
THE GALLIPOLI LETTER	39
Facsimile of the Gallipoli Letter	69

ILLUSTRATIONS

PLATE 1	Portrait of Keith Arthur Murdoch	ix
PLATE 2	Australian soldiers about to land at Anzac Cove.	5
PLATE 3	Australian troops marching across Plugge's Plateau after landing on 25 April.	15
PLATE 4	Keith Murdoch stands outside C.E.W. Bean's dug-out.	23
PLATE 5	The 21st Battalion marches up Monash Gully.	33
PLATE 6	Anglican Chaplain Walter 'Bill' Dexter on the Gallipoli Peninsula, looking down towards North Beach.	41
PLATE 7	A trench at Lone Pine after the battle, showing Australian and Turkish dead on the parapet.	51
PLATE 8	Three Anzac soldiers shelter from bursting shells in a shallow trench.	59
PLATE 9	Two men of the 6th Battalion stand behind a Garland trench mortar near the front line.	67

THE GALLIPOLI LETTER

PLATE 10 Andrew Fisher in 1916, when Australian High Commissioner in London. 77

PLATE 11 Soldiers wait to be evacuated from Gallipoli in 1915. 87

PLATE 12 A view of the long wooden pier leading to Anzac Cove, taken on the last day of the occupation. 95

PLATE 1 Keith Arthur Murdoch *By permission of the National Library of Australia, MS 2823*

PREFACE
JACK THOMPSON AM

As Australians, most of us think we know the story of Gallipoli. Some of us have even made the pilgrimage to Anzac Cove and had the emotional experience of standing there in the early morning light as the Last Post sounds. Some of us have watched Peter Weir's affecting film from the early 1980s, *Gallipoli*. Many of us have studied it in Australian history lessons at school. But all of these experiences, as worthwhile as they must be, are in a very important way incomplete.

We can never really know what it was like, or what the troops went through, though each year on Anzac Day we salute their courage and determination and celebrate the spirit of the Anzacs.

It is in this regard that the Gallipoli Letter, written by young journalist Keith Murdoch to Andrew Fisher, the Australian prime minister at the time, is so important and I believe should be read by all Australians who seek to understand what it is that Anzac Day truly commemorates. It's a passionate letter, driven by anger and a

THE GALLIPOLI LETTER

great conviction that the Gallipoli campaign had to be brought to a halt. The letter takes us directly there, into the trenches and into the minds and hearts of the men who were at Anzac Cove. Keith Murdoch vividly describes the conditions in which they were fighting and how they were feeling, describing in blunt, plain terms the hardship, fear and suffering that the blokes at the front went through.

It's a moving experience reading this letter. While the letter itself is written simply and straightforwardly, Murdoch is writing of things that he has experienced at first hand. In a way, the young Keith Murdoch was himself one of the Anzacs. It is impossible to read without a tear coming to your eye. He tells of the morale of the troops in the trenches, facing the prospect of a hard winter, with disease, miserably limited food and the prospect of being picked off by the Turkish snipers. Murdoch writes: 'It is like the look of a tortured dumb animal. Men living in trenches with no movement except when they are digging, and with nothing to look at except a narrow strip of sky . . .' And later he writes: 'You would have wept with Hughes and myself if you had gone with us over the ground where two of our finest Light Horse regiments were wiped out in ten minutes in an attempt to advance a few yards . . .' At times, the letter just breaks your heart: 'The heroic Fourth Brigade was reduced in three days' fighting to little more than 1000 strong. You will be glad to know the men died well.'

But you have to read this letter for yourself. This is the real story of Gallipoli, and we need to know it, so that every year, when we salute our soldiers, we truly acknowledge their enormous sacrifice, courage, fortitude and the mateship forged in battle and celebrated in peace; that informs the spirit of our nation. I commend it to you.

INTRODUCTION
MICHAEL MCKERNAN

He stood as far forward on the deck of the destroyer as possible, breathing deeply, his heart thumping, straining to see the land in front of him. Four months earlier, almost to the day, he had read in amazement the cable being prepared for publication in all of Australia's newspapers: the first news of the landing at the Dardanelles by Australian and New Zealand soldiers. He remembered how astonished he had been reading the cable, how excited and how proud. And now he, Keith Murdoch, was standing on the deck of a destroyer taking him to the small cove just south of Ari Burnu point, which had become known as Anzac Cove. Within minutes he would be transferred to a trawler that would take him to the wooden pier, then it was only a short walk and a jump to the shingle, and he would be at Anzac Cove itself.

He had heard the noise of battle, the crump of the artillery, while he waited impatiently on the island of Imbros, the base. Now the noise intensified as he drew closer. He heard the constant sound of the rifles, like the noise of a thousand bowlers sending down their fastest balls—'crack!'—to be despatched by a thousand batsmen in the nets at his local oval.

He thought of home as he came closer to Anzac. Of his earnest talks with his father about the bravery of the soldiers and the sad work his father had, as a clergyman, of giving parishioners the news that a son or a husband had been killed at Gallipoli. They had discussed his duty; whether he should go to the war as a soldier or continue to work as a journalist, and he had never really settled the issue in his own mind. Now he was coming to Gallipoli as a journalist on a mission.

The sea was choppy as he jumped down onto the deck of the trawler and the ragged hills loomed high above him. Those cliffs are just as high as we have been told, he thought, ever the sceptical journalist. Imagine scrambling up there under fire, in the dark, and not knowing what was to come next. And I can talk to the men who did this, he told himself. The Anzac heroes. I can walk the tracks they raced over to get at the enemy. I can see for myself what many Australians would dearly love to see. This is the most exciting day of my life, no doubt about that. I am, at last, at Gallipoli.

Keith Murdoch, journalist

Keith Murdoch was born in Melbourne in 1885, less than twelve months after his parents had migrated to Victoria from Scotland. Keith's father was a minister in the Presbyterian church, as had been his grandfather. The influence of the church on Keith, along with the influence of his Scottish heritage, was deep, profound

INTRODUCTION

and lasting. But Keith Murdoch would not follow the path of his father and grandfather into the ministry. He would dedicate his life to journalism.

•

For most of their lives the Reverend James Murdoch and his wife Helen, Keith's grandparents, had lived in the fishing village of Rosehearty in the north of Scotland. They had fourteen children, nine boys and five girls, but tuberculosis haunted the family, being ultimately responsible for the deaths of six of these offspring. In 1881, then 63 years of age and fearing further deaths, James Murdoch told his congregation that he must resign his ministry and leave Scotland. Two sons had already migrated to Victoria; it seemed logical that, if they must move, to Victoria it would be.

James Murdoch's first born, Patrick John—also a minister of the Presbyterian church in Scotland and married with one child—had accepted a call to a church in Melbourne and had already booked passage on S.S. *Potosi*. James Murdoch obtained passage on the same ship for himself, his wife, three daughters and his youngest son Walter, who would celebrate his tenth birthday on the voyage—these were all of James Murdoch's remaining family in Scotland. On 20 August 1884 S.S. *Potosi* sailed from London to Melbourne, docking there on 3 October 1884 after a journey of 44 days. The Murdochs were all travelling first class. Young Walter remembered the terrible passage through the Red Sea: 'No first class passenger went down to it [the heat]; the trouble was all in the 2nd class and the steerage. In the steerage, they died.'

James Murdoch survived less than a month in Melbourne, dying on 29 October 1884. Responsibility for the family fell to

Patrick John, minister of the West Melbourne Presbyterian church in the centre of the city. He had already found a terrace house in William Street, West Melbourne, for his own growing family. There was a son, George, born in Scotland but soon to die, then a daughter, Helen, then in August 1885 a second son, Keith Arthur; there would be four more children. In 1887 Patrick John moved to Trinity Presbyterian Church in Camberwell, a rapidly growing and prosperous Melbourne suburb. The manse attached to the church became home to Patrick's children. Described as 'broad-shouldered, straight-backed and full of Christian fun', Patrick was a demanding father with high expectations of his children.

There should have been enough money in the extended family for all their needs but the collapse of the land boom in 'Marvellous Melbourne', the bank crash and the subsequent economic depression, meant that Patrick's stipend was reduced and his mother was without income from her investments for some years. Keith Murdoch recalled it as the 'patched pants' period of his life. He was sent to the Camberwell Common School, a free government school, but was apparently bullied as a child of the manse and developed a disabling stammer. He was painfully shy and without close friends. It is a sad picture of childhood. Such was his stammer that on occasions when buying a railway ticket he would push a handwritten note through the ticket window rather than facing the ordeal of trying to say the name of his destination. Yet his home life was happy, his parents somehow recreating the atmosphere of the Scottish villages they had known in their own childhoods. Golf was Patrick John's main recreation and he and Keith often played together, the son becoming a very good golfer.

Keith finished his schooling at Camberwell Grammar in 1903, graduating dux of the school. Aware that it would disappoint his

INTRODUCTION

PLATE 2   On 25 April 1915, a party of Australian soldiers disembark their transport ship, about to land at Anzac Cove. *AWM Neg. No. J05589*

father, Keith nevertheless declined to move on to university studies and announced, instead, that he wished to be a journalist. His uncle, Walter Murdoch, just eleven years his senior, had probably planted the seeds of that aspiration. After graduating from university Walter had set up a small school for a couple of years, which his nephews attended, but during this time he was also building a reputation as a literary journalist with the Melbourne *Argus*, writing longer pieces under his own name, and anonymously contributing editorials and book reviews. Walter Murdoch clearly enjoyed journalism. His nephew Keith was fascinated and aspired to see his own name in print.

Patrick Murdoch was now a prominent minister in a prosperous suburb, with impressive and extensive connections. He introduced Keith to David Syme, the legendary owner of Melbourne's *Age*. Syme commissioned Murdoch as a 'stringer' in the Melbourne suburb of Malvern, paying him a penny ha'penny a line for published material. The commission was valuable for the *Age*, which had a limited readership in Malvern. Circulation would grow, Syme calculated, as locals read area news. The work would also prove valuable for Murdoch: on-the-job training in finding inventive ways of getting 'parish pump' material into print. Murdoch succeeded, working long hours to uncover local news stories, and he was offered a position on the *Age*'s reporting staff. The stammer persisted, however, and one can only imagine the agony Murdoch must have endured as he set about interviewing local Malvern identities. By 1908 Keith had saved enough money to be able to set off for London. In part his trip was to further his education as a journalist; in part it was to work with British experts who may be able to cure or perhaps reduce his terrible stammer.

INTRODUCTION

Keith Murdoch travelled to London with impressive references, including one from Alfred Deakin, Australia's second prime minister. But Murdoch struggled in London. A young man with parochial experience, shy to the point of inhibition and with a frightful stammer that he was reluctant to expose, he can hardly have been an attractive proposition to those hiring on London newspapers. Though he won an interview for a position on the *Pall Mall Gazette* the opportunity disappeared, Murdoch wrote, when at the final interview his 'speaking collapsed'. Lonely, with no friends and little or no work, Murdoch read widely and attended lectures at the London School of Economics. He travelled to relatives in Scotland and played some golf. Murdoch also enjoyed observing the mighty men of Empire going about their business in London. But as to work, there was none. The young man did receive treatment for his stammer and there was some improvement. It was both a physiological and psychological problem, he reported to his parents.

Writing home in late 1909 Keith asked his father to confirm a position at the *Age* with David Syme's widow, for his mentor had died in February 1908. There was no alternative for Keith Murdoch: he must again turn his face to Melbourne to try to start his career at home. Told that a place had indeed been held open for him, he returned in 1910.

It was hardly a triumphant homecoming. Keith Murdoch was now twenty-four years of age. He had never held a permanent job and he was largely unknown in the city of his birth. What advantages he had secured came largely as a result of his father's good work and prominence. Murdoch was ambitious and determined to make a name for himself and it was said that he had a high degree of self-confidence. But, as even he must have been aware, he had much ground to make up if he was to succeed in Melbourne as a journalist.

THE GALLIPOLI LETTER

Finally Murdoch's luck began to change. Melbourne was then the home of the federal parliament, created by Federation in 1901, and the centre of the federal administration. Federal parliamentarians spent months at a time in Melbourne and many members spent long hours in the parliament building, where there was a club-like atmosphere and close association between members and journalists. When Geoffrey Syme, David's son, appointed Murdoch to the *Age*'s federal parliamentary press gallery the inexperienced journalist joined this pleasant club.

Shaken by his observation of the plight of London's poor, Murdoch's political views, supported by his studies at the London School of Economics, inclined him to the left of politics just as the Federal Parliamentary Labor Party was coming into prominence. In the first decade of federation governments had been formed by coalitions of interest with no single party able to gain a majority. Alfred Deakin had described the federal scene as 'three elevens in the field'—a useless way to play cricket, and a situation unable to produce a stable government for Australia.

But at the election in April 1910 Labor became the first federal party to win government in its own right, with a majority of 43 of 75 seats in the lower house and 23 of 36 Senate seats. Labor could govern without the deals and coalitions of earlier years and Andrew Fisher, the fifth Australian prime minister in his second term in the office, became the first prime minister to exercise real power.

Murdoch and Fisher were already close. With his brother, Andrew Fisher had migrated from Scotland in 1885, the year of Keith Murdoch's birth; Fisher was then twenty-three years of age. He was a staunch adherent of the Presbyterian church and superintendent for many years of the Presbyterian Sunday school at Gympie, his hometown in Queensland. Fisher had married in 1899, and when

INTRODUCTION

he became prime minister for the second time in 1910 he had six children under the age of twelve. Even so he had time for the younger Keith Murdoch and there was a natural sympathy between the two men. They shared a common Scottish heritage, the values of Presbyterianism and a mutual concern to improve the plight of the poor and disadvantaged. They also enjoyed yarning together and Murdoch even introduced golf into the life of the busy prime minister, taking Fisher to the Riversdale course in Melbourne, where Murdoch was captain for a time. Murdoch also had good relations with other Labor ministers, particularly the attorney-general W.M. ('Billy') Hughes and the defence minister, George Pearce.

In a short space of time a transformation had come over Keith Murdoch. Perhaps it was the confidence he gained from being a man with London experience, perhaps it was the sense of being at the centre of things, on close terms with senior government ministers and the prime minister himself. Or perhaps it was that Keith Murdoch had finally grown into his own body: tall, handsome and energetic, like his friend the prime minister, Keith Murdoch was suddenly a man to be reckoned with.

Somewhat surprisingly the Labor government was narrowly defeated at the 1913 election, losing the lower house by one seat to Joseph Cook's Liberals. However Labor retained an overwhelming majority in the Senate and—almost at the time of its own choosing—provoked a double-dissolution election, the first such election to be held in the short history of Australian federal politics. Australians went to the polls again on 5 September 1914, voting for a new federal government just a month after the Empire had declared war with Germany. During the election campaign Fisher had pledged his party's full support to the war effort, to 'the last man and the last shilling'. Labor won back the Treasury benches with another solid majority in the house, and maintained its compelling majority in the Senate. Coming into office as prime minister for the third time, Fisher was now less concerned with social and economic reform than with organising Australia's response to the war. The first task was to recruit and despatch an Australian expeditionary force, acting on an offer of 20,000 men from Australia to fight for the Empire in its hour of need.

The war to end all wars

Australia had been at war at the beginning of the century, supporting the Empire in South Africa. Before that various of the Australian colonies had also despatched troops overseas, to South Africa primarily but also to remote places like the Sudan. In every case Australian or colonial governments had raised, equipped and transported the troops but had left the ultimate control of their troops to British ministers in London and British generals on the spot at the battlefield. But this was not Andrew Fisher's preference. At an Imperial Conference in London in 1910 Fisher had pushed hard for the right of those at the periphery of Empire to have some sort of voice in the oversight of imperial affairs. He wanted a permanent voice at the table for the Canadians, the South Africans, the New Zealanders and the Australians. With little support from the others and none at all in London, Fisher's initiative went nowhere but he was no doubt anxious about handing over the complete mastery of an Australian expeditionary force to the men of Empire in London. The troops were Australian and he was Australia's prime minister. Might he not have some say in their use at war and in their fate, or at least be consulted? The answer was firmly 'no'.

INTRODUCTION

Despatched from Australia in October 1914, various contingents of the First Division of the Australian Imperial Force (AIF) landed in Egypt in December and began training. The Australian High Commissioner in London, Sir George Reid, was largely responsible for this last-minute diversion to Egypt, pointing out, with force, that to expect the Australians to train on the bleak Salisbury plain in winter was reckless. Surely, Reid argued, they would suffer extreme hardship and, most likely, a severe rate of sickness.

Reid was in cable communication with Fisher about this so it appears that the Australian Government was at least consulted on the matter of the first destination of the AIF. But it knew little else about the use of its troops. In April 1915 Prime Minister Fisher was allowed to know that the Australians were on their way from Egypt to a battlefront. But he was not told where or against whom the Australians would be fighting. He was not told who would have the command of the Australians nor did he or the Australian Government have much say in any other matters relating to its own troops. It is clear that Fisher was very apprehensive about this—increasing concern for the Australian troops was causing him such worry that it impacted on his health.

Most of the Australian Government's information about the progress of the AIF came from the Australian official war correspondent, C.E.W. Bean, who had been regularly reporting back to Australian newspapers since he had sailed with the first contingent of soldiers in October. It had been an early decision to commission a single journalist, designated the official war correspondent, to travel with the troops. The government reasoned that if several reporters were credentialed to the AIF there would be too much competition among them for stories, risking the security of the enterprise and creating something of a circus.

Defence Minister George Pearce, consistent with Labor principles, asked the newsmen's union, the Australian Journalists' Association, to select one of its number as the official correspondent. The AJA invited nominations and then conducted a ballot. About twenty journalists were nominated, among them Keith Murdoch.

Murdoch had only been formerly considered a journalist since 1910 and it is a mark of his rapid progress in the profession that his nomination could be seriously considered alongside men with more extensive experience. It is a further mark of the regard in which he was held that Murdoch came second in the ballot, only a handful of votes behind the winner, Charles Edwin Woodrow Bean. Unlike Bean, Murdoch was a member of the federal parliamentary press gallery, which meant he was well known to many colleagues in Melbourne and elsewhere around the nation. It was known, too, that he had the prime minister's and defence minister's approbation, which would have helped, and that he was young and energetic. But Charles Bean had won, fair and square. Keith Murdoch was mightily disappointed.

On 8 May 1915, Fisher and his government found out—only slightly in advance of the rest of Australia—that the AIF had been diverted from Egypt to the Dardanelles where, joined with the New Zealand expeditionary force as ANZAC, they had landed on 25 April 1915 in a hazardous operation. Had the government been properly briefed from London about the Dardanelles expedition Fisher and his colleagues would have learned that British ministers, particularly the Chancellor of the Exchequer David Lloyd George, were so worried about the stalemate on the Western Front in Europe that they were looking hopefully for any second front that might create a war of movement, and bring some heartening victories. 'We need a big win,' said Lloyd George on New Year's day in

INTRODUCTION

1915 and repeatedly thereafter, 'and right now.' The War Council in London had looked at various options before settling on the Dardanelles. Ministers planned for the Royal Navy, assisted by ships from France and Australia, to force a passage through the Dardanelles by destroying the forts on the shoreline. Once the forts had been silenced, they hoped to send ships up the Sea of Marmara to threaten Constantinople (now Istanbul) and force the Turks out of the war. This would open up a route through the Black Sea to Russia, enabling the Allies to menace Germany from behind.

The adventure at the Dardanelles was immediately attractive to the amateur strategists in London—the politicians—though it was examined more cautiously by senior professional soldiers and sailors like War Minister Lord Kitchener and First Sea Lord and head of the British navy Admiral Jacky Fisher. The Australian Government was told nothing of this plan but the reluctance with which Admiral Fisher was brought to agreement would not have inspired confidence.

Admiral Fisher's reluctance was justified: the naval action failed on the day it commenced, 18 March 1915. Three ships were lost to mines and the forts sustained little damage. The man in charge, Admiral de Robeck, wrongly feared that the Turks were floating mines down the Dardanelles on the current, placing all of his ships at risk so the navy withdrew, with serious losses of ships and men and, despite urging from London, de Robeck declined to try again the next day or on any subsequent day.

Well, said the amateur strategists in London, let the forts be attacked from behind, over the land, and with that what had first been conceived as a naval action now became a matter for soldiers. The troops would now be required to overrun the forts so the warships could sail through the Narrows. But landing troops on enemy-held positions from the sea has rarely been attempted in military history and is about the hardest thing an army could be asked to do. Either London was ignorant of this, or they greatly underestimated the capacity and tenacity of the Turkish soldiers and their commanders.

The landing on the Gallipoli peninsula was a dangerous undertaking, even a foolhardy one. And still government ministers in Australia were almost completely in the dark with regard to this campaign. There had been no consultation whatsoever about the crucial decisions made in London in March and April 1915. No cables were sent explaining what would be attempted. No authorisation was sought from Australia or New Zealand for the use of troops. No justification was provided for the need for troops in support of a naval action.

So anxious was Andrew Fisher about this lack of consultation that in April 1915 he despatched the man who had been the first Australian Labor prime minister, John Christian ('Chris') Watson, to London to report back on the operations at the Dardanelles. Watson briefed Fisher in person in August 1915. Soon after the landing, though, the Australian newspapers had been filled not only with stories of the landing and the fighting at Gallipoli but also with the casualty lists that now continued, thick and fast. At first newspapers attempted to publish a photograph and a pen portrait of each Australian killed on the peninsula, but it soon became apparent that the numbers of the dead would allow newspapers to list no more than the name and unit of each man killed. Australian relatives at home were in for an anxious time. And so was Andrew Fisher who felt personally responsible for the fate of the troops that Australia had so promptly and so generously sent to the war.

INTRODUCTION

PLATE 3 Australian troops marching across Plugge's Plateau after landing on 25 April. Men in front are seen kneeling in the scrub. The troops were under fire from the other side of Shrapnel Valley. This scene is from a Turkish trench overlooking the Anzac Cove beach. *AWM Neg. No. G00907*

Soon impassioned patriots cried for more men to be recruited and trained to take the places of those killed and wounded at the front. Australia now learned to accept recruiting rallies as a part of life in wartime, learned to endure these emotional appeals for men and more men. Two of Keith Murdoch's younger brothers would enlist, Ivon in 1915 and Alan in 1916. They would serve with distinction: Ivon was awarded the Military Cross and Bar, Alan the Military Cross. Both survived the war.

Stories of Gallipoli were everywhere. Any unmarried Australian male in the right age group in 1915 would have given close thought to whether or not he should go to the war. Keith Murdoch's own home values and his love of country would likely have urged him to enlist. He had left the *Age* in 1912 to become the Melbourne political correspondent for the Sydney evening paper, the *Sun*. Now the *Sun*'s proprietor, Hugh Denison, offered Murdoch a transfer to London to be managing editor of the United Cable Service, which was supplying Australian newspapers with cable news. This was an appointment of real significance as so much of the news now affecting Australia was either London-based or London-sourced. Yet Murdoch agonised over the appointment. Should he go to London or should he join the tens of thousands of Australians who were now streaming into the army? In Victoria alone in July 1915 21,698 men enlisted. It would not have been easy to stand apart from this rush to the recruiting sergeant.

In June 1915 Murdoch wrote to Andrew Fisher seeking advice: 'I turn to you as a friend for guidance in this matter and I want you to know that I have always felt that I could joyfully perform any task you set me in the service of my country.' Murdoch recognised that the London job was important but he wrote that he knew that the war would not be won by cables but by as many men as possible

INTRODUCTION

in the firing line. The prime minister did not mince words in reply. He stated that Murdoch could perform a much better service for his country in London than in the trenches and he did not think army life would suit Murdoch. But there was more to it than that: Murdoch could be a voice for Australia in London, he believed, and could ensure that Australians would be informed about the progress of the war at the battlefronts and about the thinking of the politicians and decision-makers in London. It was one thing to have an official correspondent in the trenches, Fisher implied, but it was equally important that Australian political leaders knew what was happening in London. On your way to London, Fisher proposed, you might well visit the battlefield at Gallipoli to report back to me. Just as Chris Watson had reported on what was happening in London, Fisher believed he needed to hear a firsthand account of the situation at the Dardanelles. Officially, Murdoch's task was to report on the organisation of mail from Australia to the soldiers at Gallipoli, and on the management of the Australian hospitals in Cairo and elsewhere, both matters which had become issues of contention at home and among the troops.

'If you could picture Anzac as I have seen it'

Fisher no doubt wanted a trusted and alert intimate to give him an understanding of the campaign beyond whatever anodyne reports he was now receiving from the generals and from London. The Australian prime minister's main source of information on the Gallipoli campaign still remained the censored news reports that Charles Bean and British journalists were sending back for publication in the Australian newspapers. It was a remarkable situation which Fisher could only barely tolerate. He wanted to know if the campaign could be won; if Australian lives were being recklessly wasted for little gain; if General Sir Ian Hamilton's overall direction of the campaign was sound and likely to produce victory. He wanted to know about the morale of the Australian troops at Gallipoli and if they had all that they needed for success. The Australian prime minister, in other words, wanted the facts, straight and unfiltered, that he had every right to expect. And he knew that Keith Murdoch would give the facts to him straight.

Andrew Fisher's biographer, David Day, suggests that the prime minister had another objective in sending Murdoch to Gallipoli, that Fisher wanted Murdoch to see the frontline fighting for himself to convince himself, once and for all, that he could do better work for Australia in London than in the AIF. Murdoch was still wrestling with questions of his duty to his family and his country. Fisher wanted to keep Murdoch out of the army, writes David Day, and hoped firsthand experience of the war might well be the decisive influence in shaping Murdoch's thinking. Day's theory suggests an even closer relationship between Fisher and Murdoch, even a somewhat paternal concern on the part of the prime minister. Murdoch accepted the prime minister's commission and prepared to make his way to Anzac and to London.

•

Keith Murdoch stopped first in Cairo in August 1915, waiting for permission from General Sir Ian Hamilton, the overall commander, to visit Gallipoli. While he waited Murdoch visited soldiers in hospital wards, and began to hear rumours about the campaign. Murdoch had arrived in Egypt in late August, just a few weeks

INTRODUCTION

after a massive land offensive at Gallipoli. The offensive had been Hamilton's last throw of the dice—an attempt to capture and hold the high ground, vital if the Dardanelles campaign was to succeed. It had failed almost completely, causing a very high rate of casualties. The injured men that Keith Murdoch was meeting in the Cairo hospital wards had fought in the offensive, fresh from bloody fighting at Lone Pine and the Nek.

Charles Bean, who by now had been at Anzac for more than four months, had come to an early decision once he had experienced war at close range: he would pay little heed to accounts of the fighting coming from wounded men. This was not because these men would deliberately falsify stories of what had happened but because, under the stress of wounds and from fear for their own futures, their understanding of the situation might easily be confused. Murdoch was unaware that these wounded men might not be his best informants.

But Murdoch also spoke to Australian officers stationed in Egypt in administrative and training positions. Before he even reached Gallipoli alarm bells started to ring. Among the Australian officers there was widespread condemnation of British military inefficiency and the want of preparedness, as well as a concern about British arrogance which showed in a broad contempt for 'colonial' ways and methods of work. We Australians are definitely second class in British eyes, officers reported. There was a suggestion that British commanders were reckless in their use of the troops at their disposal, causing unnecessary casualties.

The hospitals at Cairo had shaped Murdoch's thinking before he set foot at Anzac Cove. As he toured the enormous wards holding thousands of wounded soldiers Murdoch's emotions would have reinforced the comments made by Australian officers. Could these wounds, many of them severe, permanent and life-threatening, be justified in terms of territory gained or the possibility of the overall success of the campaign? Here were the *wounded* men, Murdoch noted. What of the many thousands more who had died at the front and were now in their graves, never to be rescued by the stretcher-bearers or to find a place on a hospital ship?

'Keith Murdoch arrived today,' Charles Bean wrote in his diary on 3 September 1915. Were the two men at ease with each other when they first met on the battlefield in Bean's dugout, sheltering from the shells and bullets which were a constant at Anzac? Did Murdoch look around the dugout with some wistful, lingering disappointment that it was not his home but rather Charles Bean's? The dugout was primitive enough: a desk and chair both made out of packing cases, a sand-bagged wall for protection, a spirit-lamp, a few items of clothing hanging from nails belted into the clay back wall, a primitive camp bed and a little bit of rubbish. And men passing day and night, going about their business, maybe up to Quinn's Post or Courtney's where Bert Jacka had fought so tenaciously in May to be awarded the first Australian Victoria Cross of the war. Men talking and laughing, smoking and complaining, carrying supplies or ammunition, or stretcher-bearers on their way to another job. It took most men a couple of days on the peninsula before they could stop ducking when they heard the whizz of a shell overhead, or not flinch when a bullet thudded into one of the sand-bagged parapet walls protecting them all. It took these couple of days for men to accept the random danger of life at Anzac and the domestic nature of life there, too. Keith Murdoch had only four days on Anzac and there was much to see.

After they had yarned for a while in Bean's dug-out the official correspondent took his guest 'up to the top of this hill to see the

INTRODUCTION

view'. The photograph on page 23 shows Murdoch at Anzac in an open long-sleeved shirt rolled up to the elbows, labourer's pants with braces to hold them up, and shoes, not boots. He is holding a pith helmet made of canvas and stiff cardboard. Murdoch is tall, vigorous in attitude, hair closely cropped, earnest-looking. He was certainly not out of place among the soldiers.

The view from the top of Bean's hill must have enthralled Keith Murdoch. Men were burrowed in their thousands into the side of the cliff opposite, their home when they were not in the front-line trenches. An Anglican chaplain, Walter ('Bill') Dexter likened the scene to his days in the ministry in Gippsland in Victoria, where forest workers camped and at the end of the day would make their camp fires to cook the evening meal and boil the billy. It was just like that on Anzac, Dexter wrote. The smoke from hundreds of fires drifting lazily upwards as men began to settle in for the night. Men yarned; checked their shirts and pants for lice; repaired their clothes or read their mail. Perhaps they read an Australian newspaper or magazine, weeks out of date, but a link with home nonetheless—apparently as occupied by the footy at home as with the Turks above and in front of them.

Charles Bean was quite ill when Murdoch was on Anzac and would shortly be evacuated. Many of the men were sick, Bean told Murdoch, some of the best men too—illness had become a grave issue. There was an awful shortage of water and much of what was there was of doubtful quality and possibly harmful. There was little fresh food, Bean continued and no variety at all in the diet. As Bean was forced to lie-in for the rest of the time Murdoch was on the peninsula the question of the health of the troops was very much to the fore in their discussions. More needed to be done for the troops, Bean thought, and he feared the prospect of winter, the cold weather just a couple of months, or even a matter of weeks, away.

In the few days he had Murdoch made his way around the Australian positions at Anzac. At Lone Pine he met up with General Harold Bridgwood ('Hooky') Walker, who was commanding the First Australian Division. The Australians had just won possession of the Pine—now a bulge in the Turkish line—after ferocious fighting there from 6 to 9 August.

The ordinary soldier knew that the failure of the August offensive, except at Lone Pine, meant the continuation of the stalemate that had prevailed at Gallipoli since the second day of the fighting. Since then the Turks had settled behind their defensive line, as had the Australians and New Zealanders at Anzac and the British at Helles and now at Suvla. The August offensive—an attempt to push the Turks off the high ground and win the advantage by taking Chunuk Bair, a high point on the third ridge line, and Hill 971—was a sensible plan, indeed the only possible way that the Allies might have won at Gallipoli.

These were the crucial points in the August offensive. The fighting within the Anzac lines, lower down the battlefield at Lone Pine and later at the Nek, was merely a feint designed to draw off Turkish troops from the heights and, by weakening the defences there, to give the advantage at Chunuk Bair to the Allies. Though a feint, the fighting at Lone Pine was not any less intense. Indeed it was ferocious, conducted largely underground in the Turkish trenches across three days and nights—seven Australians fighting there would be awarded the Victoria Cross. (None of these awards dated to the first hours of the fighting because no officer survived to make a recommendation.)

PLATE 4 Keith Murdoch stands outside C.E.W. Bean's dug-out. Tall, vigorous in attitude, hair closely cropped, earnest-looking, Murdoch was certainly not out of place among the soldiers. The view from the top of Bean's hill must have enthralled Keith Murdoch: men were burrowed in their thousands into the side of the cliff.
AWM Neg. No. A05396

Hooky Walker was a British general who had replaced the Australian general William Bridges in charge of the First Australian Division when Bridges was killed by a sniper in early May. Walker had dropped back to command the First Brigade when James Legge, an Australian, took over the division but by late July Walker was back in charge. Little Hooky loved his men, Bean reported, and the men 'like [him] too. He's a man we owe something to.'

When briefed by General Birdwood, who was commanding the Anzacs, about the battle plans for the August breakout Walker had tried hard to have the attack on Lone Pine cancelled. He would lose too many of his men, he argued, for too little gain. But the general was overruled, although he managed to have the worst of the planning changed.

On 4 September, as Bean lay sick in bed, Walker talked at length to Murdoch and showed him around Lone Pine. The general had also opposed the idea of the landing in the first place—he was a man who did not blindly accept the orders issued to him. Whether Hooky Walker gave Murdoch a view of his own doubts and reservations about the men above him—William Birdwood in command of the Australian and New Zealand Army Corps and Ian Hamilton, overall commander of the Dardanelles expeditionary force—we cannot know. Murdoch was, after all, a journalist. He may well have picked up Walker's doubts and reservations. Or the men among whom Murdoch moved might well have let something slip: 'It was just murder up here, mate, when the fighting was on; sheer, bloody murder.' But we cannot know precisely what was said.

The next day Bean was sick in bed again and Murdoch headed out by himself. He roamed about, no doubt asking and listening as good journalists do. No big-noting; no mention of his commission from the Australian prime minister. At some stage Murdoch had

INTRODUCTION

also visited the British at Suvla Bay, a place easily seen from the heights at Anzac and he had been shocked by what he had found there: confusion, morale at its lowest possible ebb, failure.

On his last day on Anzac, 6 September, Bean took Murdoch to Quinn's Post, the real hot spot where the opposing trenches, Turkish and Anzac, were only metres apart. It was a place where bombs were tossed casually across the short stretch of no-man's-land, where the soldiers of both sides were ever alert for the possibility of attack. It was testing to be at Quinn's for the days or weeks that a soldier might spend there, but even for an hour or so for a keen journalist. Only brave men were ever at Quinn's.

And then he was gone. 'M left at midday', Bean reported. But his job was far from over. Murdoch went to the island of Imbros, within sight of the battlefield he had just left, to await a ship that would take him back to Cairo and then on to London. There were other journalists on Imbros taking a bit of a spell from the front line now that the campaign had settled once again into stalemate mode. Among them was the most flamboyant of all the correspondents, Ellis Ashmead-Bartlett. It was Ashmead-Bartlett who had written the first account of the 25 April landing by the Anzacs, which had been published in the Australian papers on 8 May. He had written of 'this race of athletes', and that there had 'never [been] a finer feat in this war' than the April assault; it was all thrilling stuff. But by September Ashmead-Bartlett was a disillusioned man, firmly convinced that the army must be evacuated if a mighty loss of life was to be avoided. As a first step he had decided that Ian Hamilton must be sacked: for the failure of the campaign and because he would never agree to an evacuation.

After just four days at Gallipoli Murdoch had reached much the same conclusion: that the campaign was doomed to failure. And he agreed with Ashmead-Bartlett, too, that an evacuation was the only sensible plan. Prompted by Bean, Murdoch's thoughts had turned to the coming winter and the horrors it must produce. With the failure of the August offensive fresh in men's minds, Murdoch concluded that a breakout now was unlikely and certainly impossible to attempt before the next spring, say April 1916. And Murdoch had also absorbed from Bean a real concern about the qualities of British military leadership at Gallipoli. Bean was at a low ebb, his diary shows, and in real despair about the prospects at Gallipoli. He wrote bitterly about British muddle, confusion and arrogance. Bean was also a sick man. His mood must have affected Murdoch.

So Murdoch and Ashmead-Bartlett talked and agreed with one another. 'You must let people in London know these things,' Murdoch urged, just as he would be letting his own prime minister know the truth. Ashmead-Bartlett reminded Murdoch of the commitment both had signed that required them to submit everything they wrote to the censors. 'If I wrote the truth,' Ashmead-Bartlett explained, 'it would never be passed by the censor.' When Murdoch had sought Hamilton's approval for a visit to Anzac Murdoch had written that 'any conditions you impose I should, of course, faithfully observe'. Yet briefing a prime minister, Murdoch believed, stood outside any undertaking either he or Ashmead-Bartlett had given. They could write to prime ministers without submitting to the censors, Murdoch argued. Murdoch must have resolved on this when he first applied to Ian Hamilton for permission to visit Anzac. He would report truthfully and fully to Andrew Fisher; he had a commission to do so. Murdoch now urged Ellis Ashmead-Bartlett to do the same to his prime minister, Herbert Asquith.

You are going to London, the British journalist countered, and you can tell the people in charge the truth. But it was highly

INTRODUCTION

unlikely that they would listen, argued Murdoch. After all he had only been on Anzac for four days, had seen nothing whatever of the operations at Helles and very little of Suvla. Nor had he met the most senior people like Hamilton and Birdwood, nor did he have an understanding gained by months in the field. Who in London would take him seriously? But they would listen to Ashmead-Bartlett if he were to write a letter. Murdoch was arguing a very strong case. Certainly Ashmead-Bartlett could believe that if Murdoch were to attempt to criticise the campaign in London he would make mistakes. He simply did not know enough. Supporters of Hamilton and the campaign would leap on those mistakes to discredit Murdoch and he might end up doing more harm than good. Ashmead-Bartlett agonised, eventually deciding that he would write to his prime minister—Murdoch would take the letter to London for personal delivery to 10 Downing Street.

Murdoch left Imbros on 8 September, unaware that he had already been betrayed to Hamilton, most likely by another war correspondent aghast that the two journalists were determined to circumvent the censorship to which each had freely submitted. Hamilton believed that the letter Murdoch was carrying was destined for publication in Ashmead-Bartlett's paper, the *Daily Telegraph* and that, on publication, it would cause a sensation. So Hamilton arranged with British military intelligence in France to have Murdoch stopped and the letter seized when his ship, S.S. *Mooltan*, docked at Marseilles. Indeed Murdoch was told at Marseilles that he would be arrested unless he turned Ashmead-Bartlett's letter over. Which he did.

It was an awful shock, though, to everyone involved in the seizure of the letter to discover that it was addressed not to the editor of the *Daily Telegraph* but to the Rt Hon. H.H. Asquith, 10

Downing Street, London. The military nervously asked themselves if it was right that they intercept the prime minister's correspondence. The letter was quietly lost, most probably somewhere in Whitehall. Ashmead-Bartlett was in disgrace regardless, for the potential breach of censorship. In early October, Hamilton withdrew his accreditation and told him to leave Imbros immediately. This was a tactical error on Hamilton's part. The journalist could talk his head off in London without restraint, and he did.

Keith Murdoch, though, still had a job of work in front of him. As the *Mooltan* sailed from Marseilles to London he wrote a letter to his own prime minister in Melbourne. Murdoch had not collaborated with Ellis Ashmead-Bartlett in writing their letters on Imbros but there is little doubt that the outlook of the two men was essentially the same. Murdoch's was not a formal report to Fisher, rather it was a personal letter to a prime minister who was also his friend. Murdoch had finished a first draft of the letter by the time he reached London. Over the next couple of days he polished it, either in the offices of the Australian High Commissioner or in his own office, and had it cabled to Melbourne.

Andrew Fisher was by now a sick man, exhausted by the worry and anxiety of the war. He would resign as prime minister on 27 October 1915 to become Australian High Commissioner in London. From Melbourne there was not much Fisher could do to influence events at Gallipoli but the letter alarmed him and added to his anxiety. In October Asquith cabled to Fisher warning him not to place too much faith in Murdoch's letter. He also promised to release to the Australian prime minister documents relating to the Gallipoli campaign. Murdoch's letter had already worked for Australia—there would now be some sort of flow of information.

INTRODUCTION

•

On his visit to London six years earlier Murdoch had been unknown. Now he returned as one of Australia's most prominent journalists. The United Cable Service, which he would head, had its offices in the *Times* building in London and, as a matter of course, Murdoch was introduced to the editor of the *Times*, Geoffrey Dawson, a man in a position of such influence that he probably outranked most cabinet ministers in importance. The two men lunched together and Murdoch gave Dawson a full account of his views about the campaign, the need for Hamilton's recall and the necessity of the evacuation of all the troops. The editor was appalled by what he heard, disbelieving to an extent, but horrified to hear that the campaign could not succeed. Dawson subsequently arranged interviews between Murdoch and some British politicians.

Murdoch first met Sir Edward Carson, chairman of the British Cabinet's Dardanelles Committee. The committee had responsibility for every aspect of the campaign and it needed to know what was actually happening out there, not merely what General Hamilton reported. Carson listened intently—he had been a strong supporter of the campaign at the Dardanelles. He in turn arranged for Murdoch to meet David Lloyd George, Minister for Munitions, and increasingly a sceptic about the Gallipoli adventure. Murdoch must have been persuasive because these men had originally believed in the second front. Perhaps he confused them as much as he convinced them, but out of this confusion action would finally come.

When urged by his ministers, Prime Minister Herbert Asquith, read what Murdoch had written to Fisher and was alarmed. Could this be true, he wondered? If so, hard decisions would have to be made. Apparently without consultation Asquith had Murdoch's letter printed as a paper to the Committee of Imperial Defence, immediately giving it much greater authority and significance and much wider circulation than first intended. Murdoch had cracked the facade of confidence that had enclosed the Gallipoli campaign. The Dardanelles Committee, the Cabinet, had to act.

In the course of the next few weeks Hamilton was replaced at Gallipoli by General Sir Charles Monro, who had little faith in the Dardanelles adventure. Lord Kitchener was despatched to Gallipoli to see the situation for himself and to report back, after which a decision was made to evacuate the troops from Anzac and Suvla and subsequently from Helles. The Dardanelles campaign would come to an end. The Murdoch letter played a crucial role in all of these events.

The letter

In his official history, Charles Bean described Keith Murdoch as 'a man of forceful personality, combining keen love of power with an intense devotion to his country and countrymen'. Bean approved of Murdoch's letter, although he wrote that 'the picture given in this letter was undoubtedly overcoloured, and some of its statements were not facts'.

The first point to note about Murdoch's letter is its conversational tone. Ashmead-Bartlett would not have written to Asquith in this way but Murdoch was writing to a friend and his letter has greater power because of that. 'I shall talk to you as if you were by my side,' Murdoch began, 'as in the good old days.' Murdoch

INTRODUCTION

shows that he and Fisher had closely discussed Fisher's fears for the Australians at the Dardanelles before Murdoch had set off for Anzac. Murdoch wrote of Gallipoli 'as one of the most terrible chapters in our history. Your fears have been justified.' So Fisher must already have told Murdoch that he thought the campaign was in deep trouble, strengthening the view that Fisher wanted accurate information on which he could act. Murdoch intended to reinforce Fisher's concern, perhaps even alarm.

The construction of the letter also shows how dependent Murdoch was on the talk of the men among whom he had moved on Anzac. He wrote as if he were trying to transport his prime minister to Anzac to hear the Australian officers' and soldiers' views on their predicament, to give Fisher the viewpoints of these ordinary Australians. If 'some of the statements were not facts', nevertheless, as Murdoch understood it, he was repeating to the Australian prime minister what Australian soldiers, officers and the Australian official correspondent believed to be true. Murdoch had come to listen to the Australians and then to tell the prime minister what he had heard.

This is best shown in the early part of the letter where Murdoch concentrated on the landing at Suvla Bay, which began on the night of 6 August. Among the Australians at Gallipoli a special anger was reserved for those who had designed and led the attack by the British at Suvla. There had been good sense in the attempt: in the plan, troops would have landed at points around the bay and then moved quickly to the hills ringing it. Once established on the ridge line they would have been in a good position to support the attempt of the Anzacs and others on Chunuk Bair and Hill 971, the vital points on the peninsula. Suvla's attackers would have come behind the Turks defending Chunuk Bair and help to drive them from the heights.

THE GALLIPOLI LETTER

The Suvla Bay landing was a central piece of the August offensive which was in turn the path to victory, perhaps the only path to victory at Gallipoli. For the campaign at Suvla, and the August offensive in general, the War Council in London had given Hamilton an additional four divisions. He had the men he had asked for, now he had to make the ambitious plan work.

But the Anzacs, watching the landing at Suvla as if in the dress circle of a theatre, could not believe what they saw unfolding before them. The British, in numbers, landed unopposed and then seemed to stop, seemingly making no attempt to rush forward to the hills. 'The Suvla Bay tea party' Anzacs called it, as they watched the British apparently settle down to a brew rather than rush to the hills with the advantage of surprise. Alerted to what was happening as the British assault faltered, the Turkish commanders rushed their own troops to Suvla's hills and the element of surprise was promptly lost.

There were reasons for the slowing of the British momentum, of which the soldiers at Anzac could not be aware, but Murdoch accepted their anger and contempt for the failure at Suvla and this coloured his letter to Fisher, justifying, to an extent, Bean's criticism of the letter. But Murdoch was not writing history; he was reporting what he had heard.

Much of the blame for the catastrophe at Suvla has fallen on the British general, Sir Frederick Stopford. Put simply, Stopford was too old and yet also too inexperienced for the command. Born in 1854 Stopford was 61 years of age at the time of his appointment to the Dardanelles. He had never commanded troops in battle. He had retired from the army in 1909 and was not in good health. He was selected for command at Suvla because he was the next most senior officer on the list and to pass him over would have caused unpleasantness in an army that was still based more on social class

PLATE 5 The 21st Battalion marches up Monash Gully after arriving at Gallipoli on 8 September 1915. *AWM Neg. No. A00742*

and good form than on professionalism. It was 'Buggin's turn' for Stopford. Even Ian Hamilton had urged greater vigour from Stopford in the first hours of the Suvla campaign but he was ignored. Hamilton sacked Stopford within days of the start of the fighting at Suvla but by then it was too late. Bean undoubtedly told Murdoch the sorry saga of Frederick Stopford but the letter reflects more the Australians' anger over the 'tea party' rather than an unfortunate British appointment. Murdoch describes the troops sent to Suvla as 'fresh, raw, untried troops under amateur officers'. Sending such men to battle was 'to court disaster'. Murdoch was more interested in the decisions made in London than with one elderly, failed leader.

It is no surprise, then, that the early part of Murdoch's letter to Fisher contains a blistering condemnation of Suvla. But Murdoch is exaggerating when he writes that at Suvla 'one division went ashore without any orders whatsoever' and he misunderstands when he says that another division down there had initially set off in the wrong direction. Murdoch's summary conclusion is correct, however, when he writes that, all things considered, the work of the general staff 'has been deplorable'.

Bean's influence on the letter is apparent as Murdoch moves to his next major point: that the attempt at a break out could not be resumed until spring next year and that in the meantime the troops would have to endure an appalling winter, which many would not survive. That was the anxiety in all quarters at Anzac by the time Murdoch arrived. The August offensive had failed. It could not be resumed without as many as 150,000 additional troops. And in the meantime those who were already there would simply have to sit out the awful conditions of winter: rain, wild seas, heavy snow.

This was a prospect to which Fisher needed to give the closest attention. The men were already sick, Murdoch reported, as many as

INTRODUCTION

600 soldiers a day were reporting ill. What if the force were to lose 30,000 to sickness over the winter? Murdoch asked. The 60,000 remaining 'will not be an army. They will be a broken force, spent.' This was powerful writing, and awful reading for a prime minister responsible for the health and well-being of his nation's soldiers. Fisher would need to ask himself how the Australian people would cope with the news of mass evacuations from Anzac due to sickness.

It is worth noting, too, some of the images that Murdoch used to impress his points on his prime minister. Men were already sick, he wrote, from dysentery caused by the flies. But what of the consequences, he asked, of the autumn rains which will 'unbury our dead' and add vastly to the dangers of airborne disease.

In similarly powerful prose, Murdoch had informed Fisher that 'sedition is talked around every tin of bully beef on the peninsula'. Murdoch realised that almost every soldier or officer he met had buried a good mate on the peninsula already. Australian soldiers saw themselves as quite competent to form their own opinions, to think for themselves. They had freely offered their service as soldiers to their country but they had not surrendered their capacity for independent thinking and judgement. The Australian prime minister needed to know this about his soldiers.

Sedition is a dangerous word to use about men in an army but it was an effective word to send to a prime minister. The British might have thought that Australian troops were there to be used in whatever way the British generals chose, but even the mild-mannered Charles Bean recognised the strength of independence among the Australians and railed at the arrogance and insensitivity of many of the senior British officers. Murdoch had picked it up among the Australians in a matter of days and it was another factor that Fisher had to bear in mind in his thinking about Gallipoli.

Throughout the letter there ran a thread that Charles Bean observed in Murdoch: 'an intense devotion to his country and countrymen'. In part his high regard for the Australian soldier lay in the contrast Murdoch perceived between soldiers of his own country and the British soldiers. At one point in the letter Murdoch referred to the British soldiers at Suvla as 'toy soldiers', a terrible insult.

He was on firmer ground when he wrote directly about the Australians. He wrote of the 'wonderful affection of these fine young soldiers for each other and their homeland'. 'It is stirring,' he continued, 'to see them, magnificent manhood, swinging their fine limbs as they walk about Anzac. They have the noble faces of men who have endured.' It was an implied demand that Fisher, Australian prime minister, care for these men and defend them, nourish and protect them. 'Oh,' Murdoch concluded this section of the letter, 'if you could picture Anzac as I have seen it, you would find that to be Australian is the greatest privilege that the world has to offer.'

In his book *The First Casualty* a history of war correspondents, Phillip Knightley briefly recounts the story of Ellis Ashmead-Bartlett and Keith Murdoch. Knightley concluded that, 'If the war correspondents in France had only been as enterprising, the war might not have continued on its ghastly course.' At first sight this claim seems exaggerated, possibly grandiose. But looking closely at the Murdoch letter you can see what Phillip Knightley was driving at. It was a question of telling the truth. Murdoch had a commission from the Australian prime minister to tell him truly what was happening at Gallipoli. Murdoch discharged that commission remarkably well. Yet the truths he told were terrible. That the campaign was misconceived from the start; that the leadership of the British generals was exercised overall at a level of considerable incompetence; that the campaign was unwinnable; and that the

INTRODUCTION

continuance of it would most likely cause significant loss of life, through disease and the possible increased availability of Turkish, and probably German, artillery. In Murdoch's view most Anzac soldiers would be blasted into the sea or carried across it in the hospital ships.

Murdoch ended his letter in the same personal way with which he had begun it. 'This of course is a private letter,' he wrote, 'but you will show it to George Pearce and Hughes, so I shall say nothing more than goodbye.' But it was not a private letter. It was an appeal to Australia's three most senior war ministers for the rescue of Australian troops from the dire circumstances in which they had been placed. The crucial decisions about the conduct of the campaign were not Australia's to make and these three men must have felt a degree of impotence when reading what Murdoch wrote. But the letter caused events to move as they would have wanted anyway.

The letter's real influence had been in London where the decisions were made. Hamilton had been brought home and never commanded troops in war again. The Anzacs were evacuated, the last men leaving on 20 December, just as the real force of winter set in. They were sad to go, if only because they left so many of their mates behind in graves. As the last soldiers scrambled down to the beach for the last time their boots were muffled to help prevent the Turks from hearing the footfall of these final departures. The Anzacs themselves, though, were pleased to muffle their boots so that those in their graves would not hear them leaving.

Hamilton's estimate that upwards of 50 per cent of the men would be lost in any evacuation was wildly wrong—in the end the evacuation was completed without loss. It was the most successful aspect of the Gallipoli campaign. Even so 8,141 Australians and 2,721 New Zealanders lost their lives in the fighting at the

Dardanelles. Writing in 1958 to a fellow journalist Charles Bean had the last word: 'Murdoch's letter was, I should say, the main agent in bringing about Hamilton's fall.' And a crucial agent, therefore, in bringing about an end to the entire campaign.

Sources

C.E.W. Bean, *Official History of Australia in the War of 1914–1918*, vol. II, *The Story of Anzac*, Angus & Robertson: Sydney, 1923

Fred and Elizabeth Brenchley, *Myth Maker, Ellis Ashmead-Bartlett: The Englishman who sparked Australia's Gallipoli legend*, John Wiley & Sons: Sydney, 2005

David Day, *Andrew Fisher: Prime Minister of Australia*, Fourth Estate: Sydney, 2008

Kevin Fewster (ed.), *Bean's Gallipoli: The diaries of Australia's official war correspondent*, Allen & Unwin: Sydney, 2007

Phillip Knightley, *The First Casualty: The war correspondent as hero and myth-maker from the Crimea to Kosovo*, Harcourt Brace Jovanovich: New York, 1975

John La Nauze, *Walter Murdoch: A biographical memoir*, Melbourne University Press: Melbourne, 1977

Clem Lloyd, 'Andrew Fisher', in Michelle Grattan (ed.), *Australian Prime Ministers*, New Holland: Sydney, 2000

D.J. Murphy, 'Fisher, Andrew', in Bede Nairn and Geoffrey Serle (eds), *Australian Dictionary of Biography*, vol. 8, Melbourne University Press: Melbourne, 1981

Geoffrey Serle, 'Murdoch, Sir Keith Arthur', in Bede Nairn and Geoffrey Serle (eds) *Australian Dictionary of Biography*, vol. 10, Melbourne University Press: Melbourne, 1986

R.M. Younger, *Keith Murdoch: Founder of a media empire*, HarperCollins: Sydney, 2003

THE GALLIPOLI LETTER

High Commissioner's Office,
London.

September 23, 1915.

Personal.

Dear Mr. Fisher,
The Cabinet will, ere this reaches you, have dealt with my report on A.I.F. mails and wounded, so it is no good my saying more on these subjects, other than this, that if you allow the inert mass of congealed incompetency in the Postal Department to keep you from instituting alphabetical sorting by units, 75 per cent. of our unfortunate homesick men in hospitals and at base depots will continue to receive no home letters.

It is of bigger things I write to you now. I shall talk as if you were by my side, as in the good days. In my last hurried note I could deal only with a few urgent matters affecting Australian administration, especially those concerning appointments of senior officers and treatment of wounded.

I now write of the unfortunate Dardanelles expedition, in the light of what knowledge I could gain on the spot, on the lines of communication, and in Egypt.

It is undoubtedly one of the most terrible chapters in our history. Your fears have been justified. I have not military knowledge to be able to say whether the enterprise ever had a chance of succeeding. Certainly there has been a series of disastrous underestimations, and I think our Australian generals are right when they say, that had any one of these been luckily so unEnglish a thing as an overestimation, we should have been through to Constantinople at much less cost than we have paid for our slender perch on the cliffs of the Peninsula.

The first two efforts, those of the fleet alone and of the combined forces in April–May, failed miserably mainly because London expected far too much from floating artillery. It is only now being recognised that the naval guns, with their flat trajectory, are of little avail against the narrow Turkish trenches. The last great effort, that of August 6–21, was a costly and bloody fiasco because, in addition to wretched staff work, the troops sent were inadequate and of most uneven quality. That failure has created a situation which even yet has not been seriously faced—i.e., a choice between withdrawal of our armies and hanging on for a fresh offensive after winter.

Unfortunately I was not in time for any of those big operations, but I visited most parts of Anzac and Suvla Bay positions, walked many miles through the trenches, conversed with the leaders and

THE GALLIPOLI LETTER

PLATE 6 Anglican Chaplain Walter 'Bill' Dexter stands on the track in a gully on the Gallipoli Peninsula, looking down towards North Beach. He likened scenes at Gallipoli to those he had seen in his ministry in Gippsland in Victoria, where forest workers camped and at the end of the day would make their camp fires to cook the evening meal and boil the billy. Smoke from hundreds of fires drifted lazily upwards as men began to settle in for the night. Men yarned, checked their shirts and pants for lice, repaired their clothes and read their mail, or a weeks-old Australian newspaper or magazine. *Photographer Albert Percy Bladen, AWM Neg. No. C01470*

what senior and junior officers I could reach, and was favoured in all parts with full and frank confidence. I could not visit Helles, where we have about 25,000 men and many animals and cars (armoured cars hidden helpless in trenches!). We have abandoned our intentions of taking Achi Baba by frontal assault. This was always a hopeless scheme, after early May, and no one can understand why Hamilton persisted with it. Achi Baba is a gradual, bare slope, a mass of trenches and gun emplacements, but so little did the General Staff know of its task that it expected to storm it with ease. Indeed, the General Staff sent our artillery horses and ambulance transport with our landing parties in April, as if the Australasian Army Corps could get astride the peninsula in a few days, I assure you that if our landing had been at Gaba Tepe as proposed, only a few broken remnants of our magnificent force would have reached the first defensive line. Having at last abandoned his expensive design to storm Achi Baba, Hamilton is keeping his divisions at Helles merely to hold a corresponding body of Turks. Helles is therefore the most quiet of the three zones, though even there, every yard of ground is commanded by the enemy's guns, and even the beaches are frequently shelled.

A strong advance inland from Anzac has never been attempted. It is broken, rough, scrubby country, full of gullies and sharp ridges, and it is all within easy range of the guns of the Turkish forts at the Narrows, and their artillery on Achi Baba and round about. No serious advance could be made direct inland from this quarter. Our men were I found immensely proud of their little progress on the plateau on our right—Lone Pine Plateau, Walker and Whyte thought it brilliant and wonderfully successful. But I found that we had paid 2500 men for this advance, on a short front, of 300 yards! That is the only sort of advance we can make from Anzac proper. The

THE GALLIPOLI LETTER

Lone Pine affair was partly in the nature of a holding movement, and it certainly succeeded in holding a large body of Turks, who maintained a series of fierce counter-attacks for 82 hours, during which the Suvla Bay operations were in progress.

Suvla Bay is a shallow, open indentation in the thickest part of the peninsula, about two miles and a half to the left of Anzac. The flat country leading from the beach consists mostly of a marsh called Bitter Lake, which in winter becomes a great morass. After heavy rains the flat is inundated.

On this flat in August nearly 90,000 men were landed. They were New Army and Territorial divisions. They had spent a fortnight on the water, in transports which even the most careful arrangements could not make wholesome. I was on the lower deck on one of these, and the place was putrid. The men could not be allowed on shore at ports of call. One or two regiments were given route marches, but the long spell of ship life was surely in every case weakening. Those which were to land first were given landing practice at Mudros (advanced base) and Imbros (headquarters base), but many were set ashore direct from their ships at Suvla. In addition to the ordinary weakening effects of troopships was the nervous strain of expectation of submarines. Most of the men ignored this, but I was on the Beltana when a submarine was sighted and fired at, and I know that this strain did exist.

You can imagine, then, that these fresh, raw, untried troops, under amateur officers, homesick and apprehensive, were under normal in morale when the day of landing approached. They had to be packed like sardines on the trawlers and small destroyers and vessels for the actual landing, and were kept like this for most of an afternoon and the whole of a night. Before this embarkation, they had each received three days' supply of iron rations—biscuits and bully beef—and had filled their water bottles—one bottle to each man.

Then in the early hours came the landing, when the life of man is at its lowest.

I do not say that better arrangements could have been made. But I do say that in the first place to send raw, young recruits on this perilous enterprise was to court disaster; and Hamilton would have some reasonableness behind his complaints that his men let him down, if he and his staff had not at the same time let the men down with grosser wrong-doings.

The landing was unopposed; the Turks were taken completely by surprise. But with the greatest celerity they galloped their artillery round, and opened fire also from their forts. Before the new troops had advanced any distance they were being racked with shell fire.

I am informed by many officers that one division went ashore without any orders whatsoever. Another division, to which had been allotted the essential work of occupying the Anafarta Hills, was marched far to the left before the mistake in direction was noticed. It was then recalled, and reformed, and sent off towards the ridge. As a practical man, how much water do you think would be left in those thirsty English boys' bottles by this time—after the night on the seas, and the hot march out, march back, and advance? Of course, not a drop. And yet the staff professes surprise that before noon the men were weak for want of water. The whole army suffered intensely from thirst during the next three days. There were many deaths from thirst. One general even assured me that the collapse of Anafarta Hills was due to thirst. Certainly these hot-blooded young men, scions of the thirstiest race in the world, were sent out into tropical heat with food calculated to engender fierce thirst, and without water. The divisional commanders have a just grievance against the general staff when they say that they were sent out not only with indefinite orders and without a good knowledge of the country over which they were to advance, but without water and with little or no knowledge of the few muddy wells existing in these parts.

I am of course only repeating what I have been told on all hands. But you will trust me when I say that the work of the general staff in Gallipoli has been deplorable. The general idea, that of getting astride the peninsula and cutting the line of communications connecting the southern Turkish army with its bases, was good. I understand it was Birdwood's scheme. The only criticism I have heard against it is that the great left flank movement from Anzac, which was directed against Hill 971 and Chunuk Bair while the Suvla Bay operations were in progress, was wasteful, inasmuch as the splendid Australasian troops, Gurkhas and Connaught Rangers broken to pieces in this advance could have been shipped to Suvla, and there used as the main wedge in the great effort to cross to Maidos. I discussed this criticism with our Australian staff, and found a decided opinion that the occupation of the heights assailed was essential to the success of the Suvla advance, owing to the dominating influence of Hill 971 and Chunuk Bair.

The 9th Army Corps reached Anafarta Hills, but could not maintain their position. Of the terrible manner of their retreat I need not tell you in this letter. One of our generals, who had his men trying desperately to hold on to the shoulders of 91 and Chunuk Bair (only a few Gurkhas really reached 971 and a few Australasians Chunuk Bair), was staggered to see the 9th and 10th Corps retreats, at the very time when their firm holding was essential. He was staggered by its manner, and principally by the obvious conflicts and confusions between British Generals, due I am told to the disinclination of two of them to accept orders from De Lisle, who though junior had been placed in command after the recall of General Stopford. At least two generals were recalled at once—Stopford, who had an army corps, and Hammersley, who suffered once from lapse of memory, but who was thought good enough by London for this work of supreme importance to the Empire. I am told that a second divisional commander was recalled. Diverse fates were in store for brigade commanders—at least one, Kenna, V.C., was killed in action.

The August 6–10 operations at Suvla left us holding a position which is nothing more than an embarrassment. We are about one mile and a half inland; but we do not hold a single commanding point nor one of real strategic value, and our one little eminence, Chocolate Hill, is I am assured by artillery officers, perilously unsafe. It is commanded by those crests on which masses of Turks are perched; and by screened artillery at which we cannot possibly get.

Perhaps this awful defeat of August 6–10, in which our Imperial armies lost 35 per cent. of their strength—fully 33,000 men—was due as much to inferior troops as to any other cause. But that cannot be said of the desperate effort made on August 21, after the Turks had had plenty of time in which to bring up strong reinforcements and to increase the natural strength of their positions, to take their positions by frontal assault. Some of the finest forces on the peninsula were used in this bloody battle. The glorious 29th Division, through which 40,000 men have passed, and which is now reduced to less than 5,000 men, were specially brought up from Helles, and the Mounted Division of Territorial Yeomanry were brought over from Egypt. They and other troops were dashed against the Turkish lines, and broken. They never had a chance of holding their positions when for one brief hour they pierced the Turks' first line; and the slaughter of fine youths was appalling. My criticism is that, as these troops were available, they should undoubtedly have been used in early August; and to fling them, without even the element of surprise, against such trenches as the Turks make, was murder.

One word more in this very sketchy and incomplete story of the August operations. It concerns the heroic advance of Australasian, Gurkha and Connaught Rangers troops from our left flank at Anzac. It was made from a New Zealand outpost, heroically held during the long summer months away to our left, and connected with our main position by a long sap. The N.Z. Rifles swept the hills of snipers, and were practically wiped out in doing so. Through them advanced the Wellington Brigade, other New Zealand forces, the Gurkhas and Irishmen, and our magnificent Fourth Brigade, brought up to a strength of far over 4000 for the event. The advance through broken, scrubby, impossible country in the night, despite mistakes by guides and constant bayonet fighting, was one of the most glorious efforts of the Dardanelles. There is a disposition to blame Monash for not pushing further in, but I have been over the country, through the gullies and over the hills, and I cannot see how even as much as he did could have been expected. Of course, our men did not hold even the shoulder of Chunuk Bair; but only a few hundred reached it, after most desperate hand to hand fighting, and they were swept off by an advance of more than 5000 Turks. We did not have enough men for the operation. It was a question of depth and weight; and it is sad to think that we gained our objective, all but the highest slopes; and that we had not sufficient reserves to stay there. Even if Anafarta Hills had been held in support of us, we could not have stayed on this vital Chunuk Bair with the forces at our disposal.

The heroic Fourth Brigade was reduced in three days' fighting to little more than 1000 strong. You will be glad to know that the men died well.

I must leave this story, scrappy as it is, of the operations, to tell you of the situation and the problems that face us. I will do so with the frankness you have always encouraged.

Winter is on us, and it brings grave dangers. We have about 105,000 men and some 25,000 animals—90 per cent. mules—on the Peninsula. About 25,000 of these are at Helles, 35,000 at Anzac, and the rest at Suvla. Suvla and Anzac are now joined, thanks to the brilliant Australasian work on the left flank; and it is important to remember that there are two retreats from Suvla, one to Anzac, the other by sea. These are all that remain of fully 260,000 men. Nowhere are we protected from Turkish shell. Our holdings are so small and narrow that we cannot hide from the Turks the positions of our guns, and repeatedly damage is done to them. On the other hand, the Turks have a vast country in which to select gun positions, they can change them with ease, and we cannot place them. You would marvel at the impossibility even of getting at the guns enfilading Anzac from the rights. These are hidden in an olive grove under Killid Bair plateau, and continuous efforts on the part of warships and our own finely operated artillery have been resultless. These guns have direct fire on our beaches, and frequently cause serious damage. All three positions are so exposed that one wonders why the Turks do not drive us out with artillery fire. Helles is the most secure of all; but Anzac and especially Suvla are very much exposed. Had the Turks sufficient modern artillery and shells they could make Suvla unbearable and Anzac an even worse hell than it is. Our staff has various opinions about the Turkish supply of shells, but it seems certain that there is an even greater shortage amongst the

THE GALLIPOLI LETTER

Turks than amongst us. Otherwise, the Turks are saving their shell for serious winter offensives. I must say that theory that the Turks are really short of shells did not impress me. I frequently watched them waste three shrapnel shells on the mere sport of making a trawler up-anchor and move out to sea. Of course, trawlers are occasionally hit; but the Turks cannot take such shell-fire seriously. I have seen as many as eight shells fired at two trawlers. One day recently 60 shells were placed by the right flank enfilading guns on the New Zealand beach. They caused damage and cost us 65 men; but they showed also that the Turks are not very short.

At the same time, one wonders whether the Turks are not merely playing with us, holding us there until they are helped by nature to drive us out. But that idea is discounted by the fact that the Turks have made many serious and costly efforts to get rid of us.

At Helles, the narrow cape gives some sort of protection from the waves, but it would be absurd to think that even this will permit of the landing of supplies in rough weather. Two steamships have been sunk to provide a breakwater, with the careless disregard of expense which has marked the whole of this unfortunate enterprise. These ships are even now, in the early days of autumn, rolling from side to side with the slight sea swell. At Anzac, there is only open anchorage. We have made three small wooden piers, each of them banked on one side with sand-bags as a protection for the men against shells. But against these the water barges are beginning to sway dangerously. At Suvla more ships are to be sunk. There can be no sort of safe landing place there either.

Can we keep the armies supplied with food, munitions and drafts? Many mariners and some naval men say no. I discussed this question with naval transport officers on the staff ship in Mudros, including a high and responsible official, and I am assured that the work can be done. It will mean great cost. The Navy says, in effect, that great reserves must be stored up in spells of calm weather, and that at times it may be necessary to get stuff ashore by running a supply ship on to the beach, from which the goods will have to be taken by the beach parties under the concentrated and accurate fire of the enemy's artillery.

I do not think, therefore, that the question of rough seas is vital. But certainly, should as I hope the Cabinet decide to hang on through the winter for another offensive, or for peace, we are faced with serious dangers from cold rain and snow on land. All our engineering work has been done with the idea that our positions would be evacuated by winter; and the roads are made in winter water-courses, the trenches are summer trenches, and the dug-outs mere protection against shrapnel, not against weather. All this means tremendous structural changes, and the immediate construction of good roads. And I fear that the decision has been left too late for such work to be thoroughly undertaken before the winter is upon us. No structural material had reached Anzac when I left. Nor had the food reserves amounted to more than 14 days' supplies.

Perhaps the most vital danger from weather is that, before the rains come to end all our water troubles, there will be a spell of bad weather at sea that will prevent us from getting water ashore, and our troops will have a grave water shortage added to their other trials. No water supply for a month would raise questions of the utmost gravity.

But we can overcome weather troubles at Helles and Anzac, and even at Suvla also, though General Byng asserts that he cannot keep his forces there when the Lake cuts his position in twain, unless he can bridge the immense width of this strange seasonal stretch

THE GALLIPOLI LETTER

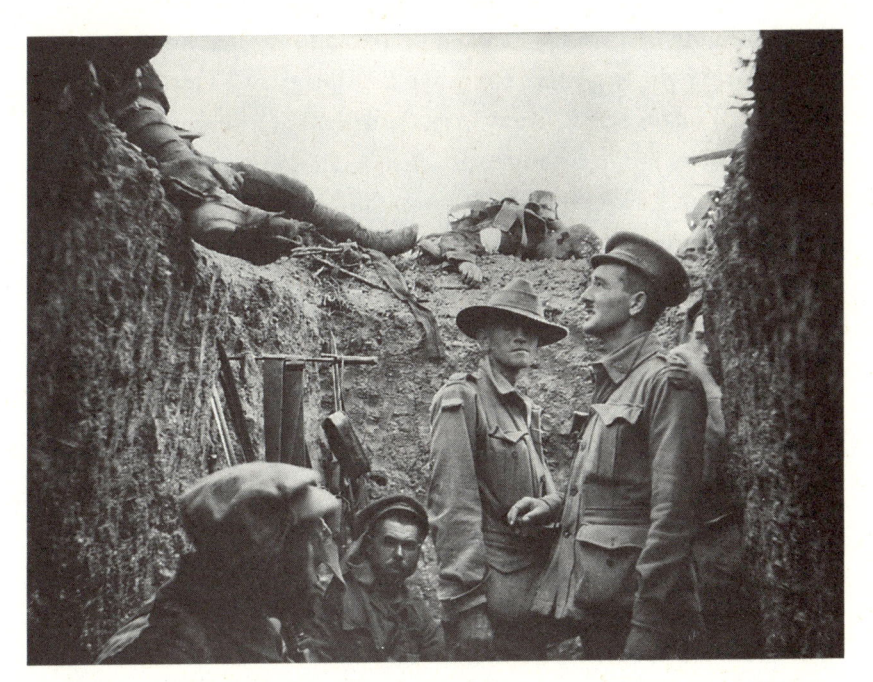

PLATE 7 A trench at Lone Pine after the battle, showing Australian and Turkish dead on the parapet. In the foreground is Captain Leslie Morshead (later Lieutenant General Sir Leslie Morshead) of the 2nd Battalion and on his right (standing facing camera) is 527 Private James (Jim) Brown Bryant, 8th Battalion, of Stawell, Victoria.

The fighting in the battle of Lone Pine was ferocious, conducted largely underground in the Turkish trenches across three days and nights. Seven Australians fighting there would be awarded the Victoria Cross, though none of these awards dated from the first hours of fighting: no officer survived to make a recommendation. *Photographer Phillip F.E. Schuler, AWM Neg. No. A02025* of water. What is more serious is the question of Turkish attacks during the cold, wet winter months.

They cannot drive us from Anzac. Of that I am sure. Australasian ingenuity and endurance have made the place a fortress, and it is inhabited and guarded by determined and dauntless men. But Suvla is more precarious. I am not prepared to say that Suvla can be held during winter. There is a grave possibility of a German army appearing on the scene. In any case, the arrival of a number of heavy German guns might be quite sufficient to finish our expedition off. Big German howitzers could batter our trenches to pieces, and we would have no reply. And remember that several of our vital positions, such as Quinn's Post, are only a few small yards of land on the top of a cliff—mere footholds on the cliffs. Whether the Germans get their guns through or not, we must make up our minds that the Turkish activity will be much greater in winter than ever before. The enemy will be able to concentrate his artillery, when he knows that we are no longer threatening any of his positions. He will be able to drag across great guns from his forts, and give any position of ours a terrible mauling. He will have great reinforcements within reach, unless the published stories, and the tales of travellers, of his large new levies are quite untrue.

We have to face not only this menace, but the frightful weakening effect of sickness. Already the flies are spreading dysentery to an alarming extent, and the sick rate would astonish you. It cannot be less than 600 a day. We must be evacuating fully 1000 sick and wounded men every day. When the autumn rains come and unbury our dead, now lying under a light soil in our trenches, sickness must increase. Even now the stench in many of our trenches is sickening. Alas, the good human stuff that there lies buried, the brave hearts still, the sorrows in our hard-hit Australian households.

THE GALLIPOLI LETTER

Supposing we lose only 30,000 during winter from sickness. That means that when spring comes we shall have about 60,000 men left. But they will not be an army. They will be a broken force, spent. A winter in Gallipoli will be a winter under severe strain, under shell-fire, under the expectation of attack, and in the anguish which is inescapable on this shell-torn spot. The troops will in reality be on guard throughout the winter. They will stand to arms throughout long and bitter nights. Nothing can be expected from them when at last the normal fighting days come again. The new offensive must then be made with a huge army of new troops. Can we get them? Already the complaint in France is that we cannot fill the gaps, that after an advance our thinned ranks cannot be replenished.

But I am not a pessimist, and if there is really military necessity for this awful ordeal, then I am sure the Australian troops will face it. Indeed, anxious though they are to leave the dreary and sombre scene of their wreckage, the Australian divisions would strongly resent the confession of failure that a withdrawal would entail. They are dispirited, they have been through such warfare as no army has seen in any part of the world, but they are game to the end.

On the high political question of whether good is to be served by keeping the armies in Gallipoli, I can say little, for I am uninformed. Cabinet Ministers here impress me with the fact that a failure in the Dardanelles would have most serious results in India. Persia is giving endless trouble, and there seems to be little doubt that India is ripe for trouble. Nor do I know whether the appalling outlay in money on the Dardanelles expedition, with its huge and costly line of communications, can be allowed to continue without endangering those financial resources on which we rely to so great an extent in the wearing down of Germany's strength. Nor do I know whether any offensive next year against Constantinople can succeed. On that point I can only say that the best military advice is that we can get through, that we would be through now if we had thrown in sufficient forces. Whyte, whom we both admire as an able soldier and an inspiring Australian leader, assures me that another 150,000 men would do the job. I presume that would mean a landing on a large scale somewhere in Thrace, or north of Bulair. Certainly, any advance against the extraordinary strong trenches—narrow and deep, like all the Turks' wonderful trench work, and covered with heavy timber overhead protection against shell fire and bombs, from our present positions seems impracticable. You would have wept with Hughes and myself if you have gone with us over the ground where two of our finest Light Horses regiments were wiped out in ten minutes in a brave effort to advance a few yards to Dead Man's Ridge. We lost five hundred men, squatter's sons and farmer's sons, on that terrible spot. Such is the cost of so much as looking out over the top of our trenches.

And now one word about the troops. No one who sees them at work in trenches and on beaches and in saps can doubt that their morale is very severely shaken indeed. It is far worse at Suvla, although the men there are only two months from home, than anywhere else. The spirit at Suvla is simply deplorable. The men have no confidence in the staff, and to tell the truth they have little confidence in London. I shall always remember the stricken face of a young English lieutenant when I told him he must make up his mind for a winter campaign. We had had a month of physical and mental torture, and the prospect of a winter seemed more than he could bear. But his greatest dread was that the London authorities would not begin until too late to send winter provisions. All the new army is still clothed in tropical uniforms, and when I left, London was still sending out drafts in thin "shorts". Everywhere

THE GALLIPOLI LETTER

one encountered the same fear that the armies would be left to their fate, and that the many shipments of materials, food and clothing required for winter would not be despatched until the weather made their landing impossible. This lack of confidence in the authorities arises principally from the fact that every man knows that the last operations were grossly bungled by the general staff, and that Hamilton has led a series of armies into a series of cul-de-sacs. You would hardly believe the evidence of your own eyes at Suvla. You would refuse to believe that these men were really British soldiers. So badly shaken are they by their miserable defeats and by their surroundings, so physically affected are they by the lack of water and the monotony of a salt beef and rice diet, that they show an atrophy of mind and body that is appalling. I must confess that in our own trenches, where our men have been kept on guard for abnormally long periods, I saw the same terrible atrophy. You can understand how it arises. It is like the look of a tortured dumb animal. Men living in trenches with no movement except when they are digging, and with nothing to look at except a narrow strip of sky and the blank walls of their prisons, cannot remain cheerful or even thoughtful. Perhaps some efforts could have been made by the War Office to provide them with cinemas, or entertainments, but of course Gallipoli is at the end of a long and costly, not to say dangerous, line of communications. This fact is the only excuse for the excess of bully-beef feeding.

The physique of those at Suvla is not to be compared with that of the Australians. Nor is their intelligence. I fear also that the British physique is very much below that of the Turks. Indeed, it is quite obviously so. Our men have found it impossible to form a high opinion of the British K. men and territorials. They are merely a lot of childlike youths without strength to endure or brains to improve their conditions. I do not like to dictate this sentence, even for your eyes, but the fact is that after the first days at Suvla an order had to be issued to officers to shoot without mercy any soldiers who lagged behind or loitered in an advance. The Kitchener army showed perfection in manoeuvre training—they kept a good line on the Suvla plain—but that is not the kind of training required at the Dardanelles, and it is a question really of whether the training has been of the right kind. All this is very dismal, and they are of course only my impressions. But every Australian officer and man agrees with what I say.

At Anzac the morale is good. The men are thoroughly dispirited, except the new arrivals. They are weakened sadly by dysentery and illness. They have been overworked, through lack of reinforcements. And as an army of offence they are done. Not one step can be made with the first Australian division until it has been completely rested and refitted. But it is having only one month's rest at Mudros. The New Zealand and Australian Division (Godley's) also is reduced to only a few thousand men and has shot its bolt. But the men of Anzac would never retreat. And the one way to cheer them up is to pass the word that the Turks are going to attack, or that an assault by our forces is being planned. The great fighting spirit of the race is still burning in these men; but it does not burn amongst the toy soldiers of Suvla. You could imagine nothing finer that the spirit of some Australian boys—all of good parentage—who were stowed away on a troopship I was on in the Aegean, having deserted their posts in Alexandria out of mere shame of the thought of returning to Australia without having taken part in the fighting on Anzac's sacred soil. These fine country lads, magnificent men, knew that the desertion would cost them their stripes, but that and the loss of pay did not worry them. How wonderfully generous is the Australian soldier's view of life! These lads discussed quite fearlessly the prospects of their deaths, and their view was, "It is no disgrace for an Australian to die beside good pals in Anzac, where his best pals are under the dust."

But I could pour into your ears so much truth about the grandeur of our Australian army, and the wonderful affection of those fine young soldiers for each other and their homeland, that your Australianism would become a more powerful sentiment than before. It is stirring to see them, magnificent manhood, swinging their fine limbs as they walk about Anzac. They have the noble faces of men who have endured. Oh, if you could picture Anzac as I have seen it, you would find that to be an Australian is the greatest privilege the world has to offer.

It is only these fighting qualities, and the special capacity of the Australian physique to endure hardship, that keep the morale at Anzac good. The men have great faith in Birdwood, Walker and Legge – not much in Godley. Birdwood struck me as a good army corps commander, but nothing more. He has not the fighting quality, not the big brain, of a great general. Walker is a plain hard-hitting soldier. We are lucky in these men. But for the general staff, and I fear for Hamilton, officers and men have nothing but contempt. They express it fearlessly. That however is not peculiar to Anzac. Sedition is talked round every tin of bully beef on the peninsula, and it is only loyalty that holds the forces together. Every returning troopship, every section of the line of communications, is full of the same talk. I like General Hamilton, and found him exceedingly kindly. I admire him as a journalist. But as a strategist he has completely failed. Undoubtedly, the essential and first step to restore the morale of the shaken forces is to recall him and his Chief of Staff, a man more cordially detested in our forces than

Enver Pasha. What the army there wants is a young leader, a man who has had no past, and around whom the officers can rally. I am hoping strongly that Smith Dorrien will not be sent out, because whether he failed or not in France, he will be said to have failed; and the troops on the peninsula must not be allowed to harbour the suspicion that second rate goods are any longer considered good enough for them.

I cannot see any solution which does not begin with the recall of Hamilton. Perhaps before this reaches you this recall will have occurred. Do not believe anything you may see about a large reinforcement and a new offensive before the winter. That I fear is impossible. If after the Suvla Bay disaster we had had another hundred thousand men to pour into the peninsula, we might well have got through. But as it is, we hold positions that are nothing more than costly embarrassments. It is not for me to judge Hamilton, but it is plain that when an army has completely lost faith in its general, and he has on numerous occasions proved his weaknesses, only one thing can be done. He has very seldom been at Anzax [sic]. He lives at Imbros. The French call him the General who lives on an Island. The story may not be true, but the army believes that Hamilton left Suvla on August 21 remarking "Everything hangs in the balance, the Yeomanry are about to charge." Of course the army laughs at a general who leaves the battlefield when everything hangs in the balance.

I could make this letter interminable, and I fear that I have only touched very incompletely on a few phases. What I want to say to you now very seriously is that the continuous and ghastly bungling over the Dardanelles enterprise was to be expected from such a General Staff as the British Army possesses, so far as I have seen it. The conceit and self-complacency of the red feather men are

PLATE 8 Three Anzac soldiers shelter from bursting shells in a shallow trench, June 1915. It took a couple of days for men to accept the random danger of life at Anzac—to stop ducking when they heard the whizz of a shell overhead, or not flinch when a bullet thudded into a sand-bagged parapet wall protecting them all. *Photographer J.P. Campbell, by permission of the National Library of Australia, an 23297150-v*

equalled only by their incapacity. Along the line of communications, and especially at Mudros, are countless high officers and conceited young cubs who are plainly only playing at war. What can you expect of men who have never worked seriously, who have lived for their appearance and for social distinction and selfsatisfaction [sic], and who are now called on to conduct a gigantic war? Kitchener has a terrible task in getting pure work out of these men, whose motives can never be pure, for they are unchangeably selfish. I want to say frankly that it is my opinion, and that without exception of Australian officers, that appointments to the General Staff are made from motives of friendship and social influence. Australians now loathe and detest any Englishmen wearing red. Without such a purification of motive as will bring youth and ability to the top, we cannot win. I could tell you of many scandals, but the instance that will best appeal to you is that of the staff ship Aragon. She is a magnificent and luxurious South American liner, anchored in the Mudros harbour as a base for the Staff of the Inspector-General of Communications. I can give you no idea of how the Australians—and the new British officers too—loathe the Aragon. Heaven knows what she is costing, but certainly the staff lives in luxury. And nothing can exceed the rudeness of these chocolate general staff soldiers to those returning from the front. The ship's adjutant is the worst instance of rude and disgusting snobbishness and incapacity I have come across. With others, plain downright incapacity is the main characteristic. I must say this of them also, that whereas at our 3rd Australian General Hospital on shore we had 134 fever cases, including typhus, with only a few mosquito nets, and <u>no ice</u>, and few medical comforts, the Aragon staff was wallowing in ice. Colonel Stawell—you know him as Melbourne's leading consultant—and Sir Alex. M'Cormick are not sentimentalists. But they really wept over the terrible hardships

THE GALLIPOLI LETTER

of the wounded, due to the incapacity of the Aragon. One concrete case is that of 150 wounded men landed in dead of night, with no provision and no instructions, at the hospital beach, to make their way as best they could to the hospital, which had no notice of their arrival. Fiaschi, de Crespigny, Stawell and Kent Hughes will be able to tell you of the absolutely shocking difficulties of this hospital in face of perpetual snubbing and bungling of the Aragon staff. While I was at the hospital a beautiful general and his staff rode in to make an inspection. Despite their appearance as perfect specimens of the general staff, I thought, we shall now get the ice from the Aragon on to the brows of our unfortunate men. But no ice appeared next day. The navy is very good, and sent some comforts and ice across, but for the three days before my visit this ice had gone astray before it reached the hospital.

I told you in my last letter of the necessity for canteen ships, and need not go into that now, but on the point of the general staff I must say that the work at the bases in Egypt struck me as on a par with that of the Aragon. Some day you will have to take up the case of Sir John Maxwell. He has a poor brain for his big position, and I assure you that our officers at Anzac have a poor opinion of the work of his lieutenant, General Spens [—a man broken on the continent, and therefore thought good enough to supervise the training of Australians—] [omitted] who is controlling our bases. The question you will have to fight out about Maxwell is this. After the last disturbance in the Whasa, when a very few of our men burnt some houses in which they had been drugged and diseased, he issued one of his famous lecturing orders, in which he referred to his regret that "even wilful murder" had been mentioned as one of the Australian crimes in Cairo. In this casual way did he blast the good name of our clean and vigorous army. I inquired as far as was possible, and could hear nothing of even a charge of wilful murder mentioned against any Australian. This order roused intense anger amongst our men. Perhaps we are too sensitive—. Our men were certainly too sensitive in their anger in the trenches when a notice was posted, I think in orders, describing how an unfortunate British Tommy had been shot at Helles at dawn for cowardice. It was almost amusing to hear our men resent this even remote connection with the Australian forces and a veiled threat of such shooting. "Such things have nothing to do with us," they said.

Our men feel that their reputation is too sacred to leave in the hands of Maxwell, and they much resent the sudden change in the attitude of the general staff, which regarded them as criminals in Cairo, and now lavishly calls them heroes in Gallipoli.

You will think that all this is a sorry picture, but do not forget that the enemy has his troubles, and that we have certain signs that his morale is deteriorating. From what I saw of the Turk I am convinced that he is a brave and generous foe, and he is fighting now for dear home, with a feeling that he is winning, and that he is a better man than those opposed to him. The Turks by the way are as generous in their praise of our men as the British and French are. Certainly the Turks are positively afraid of our men, and one of their trenches—that opposite Quinn's Post—is such a place of fear, owing to the indomitable way in which our snipers and bomb-throwers have got their men down, that Turks will not go into it unless they are made corporals. So say our Intelligence Officers. I saw many strange and remarkable instances of the humanity and courage of the Turks. Certainly his trenches are better than anything we can do, and he makes them remarkably quickly.

One word more to-day. Do for Heaven's sake make every effort to secure the recall of Sir James Porter, the Englishman in charge of the medical services. Our doctors are without exception furious with him. He made a shocking muddle of the first arrangements for transport of wounded, as I wrote you. The case against him there was unanswerable. But he has been left in charge, and his muddling continues. He lives on a luxurious yacht in Mudros. Oh, no Australian has the heart to tell of the fearful wreckage of life due to this man's incompetency. That is not a wild statement. It is truth. Even now, the great bulk of the wounded are sent to Imbros before being passed on to hospitals elsewhere. This handling aggravates sickness and wounds, yet the Generals wonder why men are sent away from the peninsula with slight sickness become worse and do not, as expected, return in a few weeks—do not return at all. Our Australian doctors have bearded Porter in his den, and talked open defiance to him, in the vain hope that he would insist on an inquiry, or lay a charge against them. We must make the best of the R.A.M.C., but we surely need not be burdened with Porter's sins. After having heart and seen something of the awful bungling of the wounded transport arrangements, one wonders how it is possible that the War Office should regard with complacency the prospect of leaving this man the very difficult work of getting sick and wounded from the peninsula during the winter. The only reason I can think of is that professional soldiers stick to each other through thick and thin.

 I hope I have not made the picture too gloomy. I have great faith still in the Englishman. And, as I have said, the enemy is having his own troubles too. But this unfortunate expedition has never been given a chance. It required large bodies of seasoned troops. It required a great leader. It required self-sacrifice on the part of the staff as well as that sacrifice so wonderfully and liberally made on the part of the soldiers. It has had none of these things. Its troops have been second class, because untried before their awful battles and privations of the peninsula. And behind it all is a gross selfishness and complacency on the part of the staff.

Much more I could tell you, but my task is done, though I shall write again next mail—I hope with better news. This of course is a private letter, but you will show it to George Pearce and Hughes, so I shall say nothing more than the plain goodbye of a friend.

Sincerely yours,
[Keith Murdoch]

THE GALLIPOLI LETTER

Letter regarding Murdoch's appointment to investigate postal facilities in Cairo:

Department of Defence,
Melbourne, 9th July, 1915.

Dear Sir,

In view of numerous complaints which have reached the Commonwealth Government regarding the non-delivery of letters and cables to members of the Australian Imperial Force in Egypt, and the difficulty experienced by persons in Australia in obtaining information concerning wounded and sick relatives, it is thought that the public uneasiness in these matters would be allayed if a report by some persons unconnected with the Forces could be obtained as to the arrangements that have been made in Egypt for these services. The Government has accordingly authorised Mr Keith Murdoch, an Australian journalist, who is on his way to England, to make enquiries when passing through Egypt with a view to furnishing me with a report upon the matters alluded to.

Any assistance which you can see your way to render Mr Murdoch in connection with his enquiries will be very much appreciated by my colleagues and myself.

Yours sincerely,
(Sgd) G.F. PEARCE
Minister for Defence.

G.O.C. in Chief,
EGYPT.

THE GALLIPOLI LETTER

Murdoch's letter of introduction to Sir Ian Hamilton:

[*handwritten at top of page*]
My dear Birdwood,
This gentleman is duly authorised—help him in any way you can.
 Yours ever,
 Ian Hamilton
 2.9.15

Department of Defence.
Melbourne. 13th July 1915.

Dear Sir Ian Hamilton,
 Mr Keith Murdoch, Pressman of Sydney and Melbourne, is on his way to London to fill an appointment there and has been asked by this Government to make certain enquiries in connexion with postal facilities at the Base in Egypt, and as to the disposition of wounded. It might just happen that circumstances will favour him to the extent of meeting yourself and, in case this should be so, I have much pleasure in giving him this letter of introduction.
 Yours sincerely,
 G.F. Pearce

General Sir Ian Hamilton. G.C.B. D.S.O.
General Officer Commanding in Chief.
Mediterranean Expeditionary Force.

PLATE 9 Two men of the 6th Battalion stand behind a Garland trench mortar near the front line. Note the feet of a resting soldier and some items of kit in the foreground. *Photographer John David Rogers, AWM Neg. No. P02276.009*

THE GALLIPOLI LETTER

A letter from Keith Murdoch to Prime Minister H.H. Asquith:

Arundel Hotel,
Victoria Embankment.
September 25, 1915.

The Right Honourable H. H. Asquith, P.C., M.P.,
Prime Minister.

Dear Sir,

    Mr. Lloyd George has suggested to me that I should place at your disposal whatever knowledge I gained of the Dardanelles operations while an Australian civilian representative there.

    I therefore take the liberty of sending to you a copy of a private letter I have addressed to Mr. Fisher, in conformance with his request that I should write him fully on the subject.

    This letter was, of course, intended only for Commonwealth Ministers, and contains references which will have no interest to you. But I feel justified in sending it to you, because if it adds one iota to your information, or presents the Australian point of view, it will be of service in this most critical moment.

    I write with diffidence, and only at Mr. Lloyd George's request. In any case, you will know that my motive is one of affectionate regard for our soldiers' interests.

    I have the honour to be,
    Your obedient servant,
    KM

FACSIMILE OF THE GALLIPOLI LETTER

FACSIMILE OF THE GALLIPOLI LETTER

High Commissioner's Office,
London.

September 23, 1915.

Personal.

Dear Mr. Fisher,

The Cabinet will, ere this reaches you, have dealt with my report on A.I.F. mails and wounded, so it is no good my saying more on these subjects, other than this, that if you allow the inert mass of congealed incompetency in the Postal Department to keep you from instituting alphabetical sorting by units, 75 per cent. of our unfortunate homesick men in hospitals and at base depots will continue to receive no home letters. (1)

It is of bigger things I write you now. I shall talk as if you were by my side, as in the good days. In my last hurried note I could deal only with a few urgent matters affecting Australian administration, especially those concerning appointments of senior officers and treatment of wounded. (2)

I now write of the unfortunate Dardanelles expedition, in the light of what knowledge I could gain on the spot, on the lines of communication, and in Egypt.

It is undoubtedly one of the most terrible chapters in our history. Your fears have been justified. I have not military knowledge to be able to say whether the enterprise ever had a chance of succeeding. Certainly there has been a series of disastrous underestimations, and I think our Australian generals are right when they say, that had any one of these been luckily so unEnglish a thing as an overestimation, we should have been through to Constantinople

Mr. Fisher. 2.

at much less cost than we have paid for our slender perch on the cliffs of the Peninsula.

The first two efforts, those of the fleet alone and of the combined forces in April-May, failed miserably mainly because London expected far too much from floating artillery. It is only now being recognised that the naval guns, with their flat trajectory, are of little avail against the narrow Turkish trenches. The last great effort, that of August 6-21, was a costly and bloody fiasco because, in addition to wretched staff work, the troops sent were inadequate and of most uneven quality.(3) That failure has created a situation which even yet has not been seriously faced - i.e., a choice between withdrawal of our armies and hanging on for a fresh offensive after winter.

Unfortunately I was not in time for any of these big operations, but I visited most parts of Anzac and Suvla Bay positions, walked many miles through the trenches, conversed with the leaders and what senior and junior officers I could reach, and was favoured in all parts with full and frank confidence. I could not visit Helles, where we have about 25,000 men and many animals and cars (armoured cars hidden helpless in trenches !). We have abandoned our intentions of taking Achi Baba by frontal assault. This was always a hopeless scheme, after early May, and no one can understand why Hamilton persisted with it. Achi Baba is a gradual, bare slope, a mass of trenches and gun emplacements, but so little did the General Staff know of its task that it expected to storm it with ease. Indeed, the General Staff sent our artillery horses and ambulance transport with our landing parties in April, as if the Australasian

FACSIMILE OF THE GALLIPOLI LETTER

Mr. Fisher. 3.

Army Corps could get astride the peninsula in a few days, I assure you that if our landing had been at Gaba Tepe as proposed, only a few broken remnants of our magnificent force would have reached the first defensive line. Having at last abandoned his expensive design to storm Achi Baba, Hamilton is keeping his divisions at Helles merely to hold a corresponding body of Turks. Helles is therefore the most quiet of the three zones, though even there, every yard of ground is commanded by the enemy's guns, and even the beaches are frequently shelled.

    A strong advance inland from Anzac has never been attempted. It is broken, rough, scrubby country, full of gullies and sharp ridges, and it is all within easy range of the guns of the Turkish forts at the Narrows, and their artillery on Achi Baba and round about. No serious advance could be made direct inland from this quarter. Our men were I found immensely proud of their little progress on the plateau on our right - Lone Pine Plateau, Walker and Whyte thought it brilliant and wonderfully successful. But I found that we had paid 2500 men for this advance, on a short front, of 300 yards ! That is the only sort of advance we can make from Anzac proper. The Lone Pine affair was partly in the nature of a holding movement, and it certainly succeeded in holding a large body of Turks, who maintained a series of fierce counter-attacks for 82 hours, during which the Suvla Bay operations were in progress.

    Suvla Bay is a shallow, open indentation in the thickest part of the peninsula, about two miles and a half to the left of Anzac. The flat country leading from the beach consists mostly of a marsh called Bitter Lake, which in winter becomes a

THE GALLIPOLI LETTER

Mr. Fisher.   4.

great morass. After heavy rains the flat is inundated.

On this flat in August nearly 90,000 men were landed. They were New Army and Territorial divisions. They had spent a fortnight on the water, in transports which even the most careful arrangements could not make wholesome. I was on the lower deck on one of these, and the place was putrid. The men could not be allowed on shore at ports of call.   One or two regiments were given route marches, but the long spell of ship life was surely in every case weakening. Those which were to land first were given landing practice at Mudros (advanced base) and Imbros (headquarters base), but many were set ashore direct from their ships at Suvla. In addition to the ordinary weakening effects of troopships was the nervous strain of expectation of submarines. Most of the men ignored this, but I was on the Beltana when a submarine was sighted and fired at, and I know that this strain did exist.

You can imagine, then, that these fresh, raw, untried troops, under amateur officers, homesick and apprehensive, were under normal in morale when the day of landing approached. They had to be packed like sardines on the trawlers and small destroyers and vessels for the actual landing, and were kept like this for most of an afternoon and the whole of a night. Before this embarkation, they had each received three days' supply of iron rations - biscuits and bully beef - and had filled their water bottles - one bottle to each man.

Then in the early hours came the landing, when the life of man is at its lowest.

Mr. Fisher. 5.

I do not say that better arrangements could have been made. But I do say that in the first place to send raw, young recruits on this perilous enterprise was to court disaster; and Hamilton would have some reasonableness behind his complaints that his men let him down, if he and his staff had not at the same time let the men down with grosser wrong-doings.

The landing was unopposed; the Turks were taken completely by surprise. But with great celerity they galloped their artillery round, and opened fire also from their forts. Before the new troops had advanced any distance they were being racked with shell fire.

I am informed by many officers that one division went ashore without any orders whatsoever. Another division, to which had been allotted the essential work of occupying the Anafarta Hills, was marched far to the left before the mistake in direction was noticed. It was then recalled, and reformed, and sent off towards the ridge. As a practical man, how much water do you think would be left in these thirsty English boys' bottles by this time - after the night on the seas, and the hot march out, march back, and advance ? Of course, not a drop. And yet the staff professes surprise that before noon the men were weak for want of water. The whole army suffered intensely from thirst during the next three days. There were many deaths from thirst. One general even assured me that the collapse on Anafarta Hills was due to thirst. Certainly these hot-blooded young men, scions of the thirstiest race in the world, were sent out into tropical heat with food calculated to engender fierce thirst, and without water. The divisional commanders

Mr. Fisher. 6.

have a just grievance against the general staff when they say that they were sent out not only with indefinite orders and without a good knowledge of the country over which they were to advance, but without water and with little or no knowledge of the few muddy wells existing in these parts.

I am of course only repeating what I have been told on all hands. But you will trust me when I say that the work of the general staff in Gallipoli has been deplorable. The general idea, that of getting astride the peninsula and cutting the line of communications connecting the southern Turkish army with its bases, was good. I understand it was Birdwood's scheme. The only criticism I have heard against it is that the great left flank movement from Anzac, which was directed against Hill 971 and Chunuk Bair while the Suvla Bay operations were in progress, was wasteful, inasmuch as the splendid Australasian troops, Gurkhas and Connaught Rangers broken to pieces in this advance could have been shipped to Suvla, and there used as the main wedge in the great effort to cross to Maidos. I discussed this criticism with our Australian staff, and found a decided opinion that the occupation of the heights assailed was essential to the success of the Suvla advance, owing to the dominating influence of Hill 971 and Chunuk Bair.

The 9th Army Corps reached Anafarta Hills, but could not maintain their position. Of the terrible manner of their retreat I need not tell you in this letter. One of our generals, who had his men trying desperately to hold on to the shoulders of 971 and Chunuk Bair (only a few Gurkhas really reached 971 and a few Australasians Chunuk Bair), was staggered to see the 9th and 10th

FACSIMILE OF THE GALLIPOLI LETTER

PLATE 10 Andrew Fisher in 1916, then Australian High Commissioner in London and former prime minister of Australia. He and Keith Murdoch were at one time close—Fisher even demonstrated a paternal concern for Murdoch in advising him to serve Australia's interest as a journalist, and not as a soldier. *Image courtesy of the State Library of South Australia, SLSA: PRG 280/1/3/289*

Mr. Fisher. 7.

Corps retreats, at the very time when their firm holding was essential. He was staggered by its manner, and principally by the obvious conflicts and confusions between British Generals, due I am told to the disinclination of two of them to accept orders from De Lisle, who though junior had been placed in command after the recall of General Stopford. At least two generals were recalled at once - Stopford, who had an army corps, and Hammersley, who for two years was under lock and key through lapse of memory, but who was thought good enough by London for this work of supreme importance to the Empire. I am told that a second divisional commander was recalled. Diverse fates were in store for brigade commanders - at least one, Kenna, V.C., was killed in action.

The August 6-10 operations at Suvla left us holding a position which is nothing more than an embarrassment. We are about one mile and a half inland; but we do not hold a single commanding point nor one of real strategic value, and our one little eminence, Chocolate Hill, is I am assured by artillery officers, perilously unsafe. It is commanded by those crests on which masses of Turks are perched; and by screened artillery at which we cannot possibly get.

Perhaps this awful defeat of August 6-10, in which our Imperial armies lost 35 per cent. of their strength - fully 33,000 men - was due as much to inferior troops as to any other cause. But that cannot be said of the desperate effort made on August 21, after the Turks had had plenty of time in which to bring up strong reinforcements and to increase the natural strength of their positions, to take their positions by frontal assault. Some

FACSIMILE OF THE GALLIPOLI LETTER

Mr. Fisher. 8.

of the finest forces on the peninsula were used in this bloody battle. The glorious 29th Division, through which 40,000 men have passed, and which is now reduced to less than 5,000 men, were specially brought up from Helles, and the Mounted Division of Territorial Yeomanry were brought over from Egypt. They and other troops were dashed against the Turkish lines, and broken. They never had a chance of holding their positions when for one brief hour they pierced the Turks' first line ; and the slaughter of fine youths was appalling. My criticism is that, as these troops were available, they should undoubtedly have been used in early August; and to fling them, without even the element of surprise, against such trenches as the Turks make, was murder.

        One word more in this very sketchy and incomplete story of the August operations. It concerns the heroic advance of Australasian, Gurkha and Connaught Rangers troops from our left flank at Anzac. It was made from a New Zealand outpost, heroically held during the long summer months away to our left, and connected with our main position by a long sap. The N.Z. Rifles swept the hills of snipers, and were practically wiped out in doing so. Through them advanced the Wellington Brigade, other New Zealand forces, the Gurkhas and Irishmen, and our magnificent Fourth Brigade, brought up to a strength of far over 4000 for the event. The advance through broken, scrubby, impossible country in the night, despite mistakes by guides and constant bayonet fighting, was one of the most glorious efforts of the Dardanelles. There is a disposition to blame Monash for not pushing further in, but I have been over the country, through the gullies and over the hills, and I cannot see how even as

Mr. Fisher.   9.

much as he did could have been expected. Of course, our men did not hold even the shoulder of Chunuk Bair; but only a few hundred reached it, after most desperate hand to hand fighting, and they were swept off by an advance of more than 5000 Turks. We did not have enough men for the operation. It was a question of depth and weight; and it is sad to think that we gained our objective, all but the highest slopes; and that we had not sufficient reserves to stay there. Even if Anafarta Hills had been held in support of us, we could not have stayed on this vital Chunuk Bair with the forces at our disposal.

The heroic Fourth Brigade was reduced in three days' fighting to little more than 1000 strong. You will be glad to know that the men died well.

I must leave this story, scrappy as it is, of the operations, to tell you of the situation and the problems that face us. I will do so with the frankness you have always encouraged.

Winter is on us, and it brings grave dangers. We have about 105,000 men and some 25,000 animals - 90 per cent. mules - on the Peninsula. About 25,000 of these are at Helles, 35,000 at Anzac, and the rest at Suvla. Suvla and Anzac are now joined, thanks to the brilliant Australasian work on the left flank; and it is important to remember that there are two retreats from Suvla, one to Anzac, the other by sea. These are all that remain of fully 260,000 men. Nowhere are we protected from Turkish shell. Our holdings are so small and narrow that we cannot hide from the Turks the positions of our guns, and repeatedly damage is done to them. On the other hand, the Turks have a vast country in which to select

Mr. Fisher. 10.

gun positions, they can change them with ease, and we cannot place them. You would marvel at the impossibility even of getting at the guns enfilading Anzac from the right. These are hidden in an olive grove under Killid Bair plateau, and continuous efforts on the part of warships and our own finely operated artillery have been resultless. These guns have direct fire on our beaches, and frequently cause serious damage. All three positions are so exposed that one wonders why the Turks do not drive us out with artillery fire. Helles is the most secure of all; but Anzac and especially Suvla are very much exposed. Had the Turks sufficient modern artillery and shells they could make Suvla unbearable and Anzac an even worse hell than it is. Our staff has various opinions about the Turkish supply of shells, but it seems certain that there is an even greater shortage amongst the Turks than amongst us. Otherwise, the Turks are saving their shell for serious winter offensives. I must say that the theory that the Turks are really short of shells did not impress me. I frequently watched them waste three shrapnel shells on the mere sport of making a trawler up-anchor and move out to sea. Of course, trawlers are occasionally hit; but the Turks cannot take such shell-fire seriously. I have seen as many as eight shells fired at two trawlers. One day recently 60 shells were placed by the right flank enfilading guns on the New Zealand beach. They caused damage and cost us 65 men; but they showed also that the Turks are not very short.

At the same time, one wonders whether the Turks are not merely playing with us, holding us there until they are helped by nature to drive us out. But that idea is discounted by the

Mr. Fisher. 11.

fact that the Turks have made many serious and costly efforts to get rid of us.

At Helles, the narrow cape gives some sort of protection from the waves, but it would be absurd to think that even this will permit of the landing of supplies in rough weather. Two steamships have been sunk to provide a breakwater, with the careless disregard of expense which has marked the whole of this unfortunate enterprise. These ships are even now, in the early days of autumn, rolling from side to side with the slight sea swell. At Anzac, there is only open anchorage. We have made three small wooden piers, each of them banked on one side with sand-bags as a protection for the men against shells. But against these the water barges are beginning to sway dangerously. At Suvla more ships are to be sunk. There can be no sort of safe landing place there either.

Can we keep the armies supplied with food, munitions and drafts ? Many mariners and some naval men say no. I discussed this question with naval transport officers on the staff ship in Mudros, including a high and responsible official, and I am assured that the work can be done. It will mean great cost. The Navy says, in effect, that great reserves must be stored up in spells of calm weather, and that at times it may be necessary to get stuff ashore by running a supply ship on to the beach, from which the goods will have to be taken by the beach parties under the concentrated and accurate fire of the enemy's artillery.

I do not think, therefore, that the question of rough seas is vital. But certainly, should as I hope the Cabinet decide to hang on through the winter for another offensive, or for peace, we are faced with serious dangers from cold rain and snow on

Mr. Fisher. 12.

land. All our engineering work has been done with the idea that our positions would be evacuated by winter; and the roads are made in winter water-courses, the trenches are summer trenches, and the dug-outs mere protection against shrapnel, not against weather. All this means tremendous structural changes, and the immediate construction of good roads. And I fear that the decision has been left too late for such work to be thoroughly undertaken before the winter is upon us. No structural material had reached Anzac when I left. Nor had the food reserves amounted to more than 14 days' supplies.

Perhaps the most vital danger from weather is that, before the rains come to end all our water troubles, there will be a spell of bad weather at sea that will prevent us from getting water ashore, and our troops will have a grave water shortage added to their other trials. No water supply for a month would raise questions of the utmost gravity.

But we can overcome weather troubles at Helles and Anzac, and even at Suvla also, though General Byng asserts that he cannot keep his forces there when the Lake cuts his positions in twain, unless he can bridge the immense width of this strange seasonal stretch of water. What is more serious is the question of Turkish attacks during the cold, wet winter months.

They cannot drive us from Anzac. Of that I am sure. Australasian ingenuity and endurance have made the place a fortress, and it is inhabited and guarded by determined and dauntless men. But Suvla is more precarious. I am not prepared to say that Suvla can be held during winter. There is a grave possibility of a

Mr. Fisher. 13.

German army appearing on the scene. In any case, the arrival of a number of heavy German guns might be quite sufficient to finish our expedition off. Big German howitzers could batter our trenches to pieces, and we would have no reply. And remember that several of our vital positions, such as Quinn's Post, are only a few small yards of land on the top of a cliff - mere footholds on the cliffs. Whether the Germans get their guns through or not, we must make up our minds that the Turkish activity willbe much greater in winter than ever before. The enemy will be able to concentrate his artillery, when he knows that we are no longer threatening any of his positions. He will be able to drag across great guns from his forts, and give any position of ours a terrible mauling. He will have great reinforcements within reach, unless the published stories, and the tales of travellers, of his large new levies are quite untrue.

We have to face not only this menace, but the frightful weakening effect of sickness. Already the flies are spreading dysentery to an alarming extent, and the sick rate would astonish you. It cannot be less than 600 a day. We must be evacuating fully 1000 sick and wounded men every day. When the autumn rains come and unbury our dead, now lying under a light soil in our trenches, sickness must increase. Even now the stench in many of our trenches is sickening. Alas, the good human stuff that there lies buried, the brave hearts still, the sorrow in our hard-hit Australian households.

Supposing we lose only 30,000 during winter from sickness. That means that when spring comes we shall have about 60,000 men left. But they will not be an army. They will be a broken force, spent. A winter in Gallipoli will be a winter under severe strain,

FACSIMILE OF THE GALLIPOLI LETTER

<u>Mr. Fisher.</u>   14.

under shell-fire, under the expectation of attack, and in the anguish which is inescapable on this shell-torn spot. The troops will in reality be on guard throughout the winter. They will stand to arms throughout long and bitter nights. Nothing can be expected from them when at last the normal fighting days come again. The new offensive must then be made with a huge army of new troops. Can we get them ? Already the complaint in France is that we cannot fill the gaps, that after an advance our thinned ranks cannot be replenished.

But I am not a pessimist, and if there is really military necessity for this awful ordeal, then I am sure the Australian troops will face it. Indeed, anxious though they are to leave the dreary and sombre scene of their wreckage, the Australian divisions would strongly resent the confession of failure that a withdrawal would entail. They are dispirited, they have been through such warfare as no army has seen in any part of the world, but they are game to the end.

On the high political question of whether good is to be served by keeping the armies in Gallipoli, I can say little, for I am uninformed. Cabinet Ministers here impress me with the fact that a failure in the Dardanelles would have most serious results in India. Persia is giving endless trouble, and there seems to be little doubt that India is ripe for trouble. Nor do I know whether the appalling outlay in money on the Dardanelles expedition, with its huge and costly line of communications, can be allowed to continue without endangering those financial resources on which we rely to so great an extent in the wearing down of Germany's strength. Nor do I know whether any offensive next year against Constantinople can succeed.

Mr. Fisher.   15.

On that point I can only say that the best military advice is that we can get through, that we would be through now if we had thrown in sufficient forces. Whyte, whom we both admire as an able soldier (8) and an inspiring Australian leader, assures me that another 150,000 men would do the job. I presume that would mean a landing on a large scale somewhere in Thrace, or north of Bulair. Certainly, any advance against the extraordinary strong trenches - narrow and deep, like all the Turks' wonderful trench work, and covered with heavy timber overhead protection against shell fire and bombs, from our present positions seems impracticable. You would have wept with Hughes and myself if you had gone with us over the ground where two of our finest Light Horse regiments were wiped out in ten minutes in a brave effort to advance a few yards to Dead Men's Ridge. (9) We lost five hundred men, squatter's sons and farmer's sons, on that terrible spot. Such is the cost of so much as looking out over the top of our trenches.

And now one word about the troops. No one who sees them at work in trenches and on beaches and in saps can doubt that their morale is very severely shaken indeed. It is far worse at Suvla, although the men there are only two months from home, than anywhere else. The spirit at Suvla is simply deplorable. The men have no confidence in the staff, and to tell the truth they have little confidence in London. I shall always remember the stricken face of a young English lieutenant when I told him he must make up his mind for a winter campaign. He had had a month of physical and mental torture, and the prospect of a winter seemed more than he could bear. But his greatest dread was that the London authorities would not begin until too late to send winter provisions. All the

PLATE 11 Soldiers wait to be evacuated from Gallipoli in 1915. *By permission of the National Library of Australia, 24598329*

Mr. Fisher. 16.

new army is still clothed in tropical uniforms, and when I left, London was still sending out drafts in thin "shorts". Everywhere one encountered the same fear that the armies would be left to their fate, and that the many shipments of materials, food and clothing required for winter would not be despatched until the weather made their landing impossible. This lack of confidence in the authorities arises principally from the fact that every man knows that the last operations were grossly bungled by the general staff, and that Hamilton has led a series of armies into a series of cul-de-sacs. You would hardly believe the evidence of your own eyes at Suvla. You would refuse to believe that these men were really British soldiers. So badly shaken are they by their miserable defeats and by their surroundings, so physically affected are they by the lack of water and the monotony of a salt beef and rice diet, that they show an atrophy of mind and body that is appalling. I must confess that in our own trenches, where our men have been kept on guard for abnormally long periods, I saw the same terrible atrophy. You can understand how it arises. It is like the look of a tortured dumb animal. Men living in trenches with no movement except when they are digging, and with nothing to look at except a narrow strip of sky and the blank walls of their prisons, cannot remain cheerful or even thoughtful. Perhaps some efforts could have been made by the War Office to provide them with cinemas, or entertainments, but of course Gallipoli is at the end of a long and costly, not to say dangerous, line of communications. This fact is the only excuse for the excess of bully-beef feeding.

   The physique of those at Suvla is not to be compared

Mr. Fisher.   17.

with that of the Australians. Nor is their intelligence. I fear also that the British physique is very much below that of the Turks. Indeed, it is quite obviously so. Our men have found it impossible to form a high opinion of the British K. men and territorials. They are merely a lot of childlike youths without strength to endure or brains to improve their conditions. I do not like to dictate this sentence, even for your eyes, but the fact is that after the first day at Suvla an order had to be issued to officers to shoot without mercy any soldiers who lagged behind or loitered in an advance. The Kitchener army showed perfection in manoeuvre training - they kept a good line on the Suvla plain - but that is not the kind of training required at the Dardanelles, and it is a question really whether the training has been of the right kind. All this is very dismal, and they are of course only my impressions. But every Australian officer and man agrees with what I say.

    At Anzac the morale is good. The men are thoroughly dispirited, except the new arrivals. They are weakened sadly by dysentery and illness. They have been overworked, through lack of reinforcements. And as an army of offence they are done. Not one step can be made with the first Australian division until it has been completely rested and refitted. But it is having only one month's rest at Mudros. The New Zealand and Australian Division (Godley's) also is reduced to only a few thousand men and has shot its bolt. But the men of Anzac would never retreat. And the one way to cheer them up is to pass the word that the Turks are going to attack, or that an assault by our forces is being planned. The great fighting spirit of the race is still burning in these men; but it does not burn amongst the toy

Mr. Fisher. 18.

soldiers of Suvla. You could imagine nothing finer than the spirit of some Australian boys - all of good parentage - who were stowed away on a troopship I was on in the Aegean, having deserted their posts in Alexandria out of mere shame of the thought of returning to Australia without having taken part in the fighting on Anzac's sacred soil. These fine country lads, magnificent men, knew that the desertion would cost them their stripes, but that and the loss of pay did not worry them. How wonderfully generous is the Australian soldier's view of life! These lads discussed quite fearlessly the prospects of their deaths, and their view was, " It is no disgrace for an Australian to die beside good pals in Anzac, where his best pals are under the dust."

But I could pour into your ears so much truth about the grandeur of our Australian army, and the wonderful affection of these fine young soldiers for each other and their homeland, that your Australianism would become a more powerful sentiment than before. It is stirring to see them, magnificent manhood, swinging their fine limbs as they walk about Anzac. They have the noble faces of men who have endured. Oh, if you could picture Anzac as I have seen it, you would find that to be an Australian is the greatest privilege the world has to offer.

It is only these fighting qualities, and the special capacity of the Australian physique to endure hardship, that keep the morale at Anzac good. The men have great faith in Birdwood, Walker and Legge - not much in Godley. Birdwood struck me as a good army corps commander, but nothing more. He has not the fighting quality, nor the big brain, of a great general. Walker is a plain hard-hitting

FACSIMILE OF THE GALLIPOLI LETTER

Mr. Fisher.   19.

soldier. We are lucky in these men. But for the general staff, and I fear for Hamilton, officers and men have nothing but contempt. They express it fearlessly. That however is not peculiar to Anzac. Sedition is talked round every tin of bully beef on the peninsula, and it is only loyalty that holds the forces together. Every returning troopship, every section of the line of communications, is full of the same talk. I like General Hamilton, and found him exceedingly kindly. I admire him as a journalist. But as a strategist he has completely failed. Undoubtedly, the essential and first step to restore the morale of the shaken forces is to recall him and his Chief of Staff, a man more cordially detested in our forces than Enver Pasha. What the army there wants is a young leader, a man who has had no past, and around whom the officers can rally. I am hoping strongly that Smith Dorrien will not be sent out, because whether he failed or not in France, he will be said to have failed; and the troops on the peninsula must not be allowed to harbour the suspicion that second rate goods are any longer considered good enough for them.

I cannot see any solution which does not begin with the recall of Hamilton. Perhaps before this reaches you this recall will have occurred. Do not believe anything you may see about a large reinforcement and a new offensive before the winter. That I fear is impossible. If after the Suvla Bay disaster we had had another hundred thousand men to pour into the peninsula, we might well have got through. But as it is, we hold positions that are nothing more than costly embarrassments. It is not for me to judge Hamilton, but it is plain that when an army has completely lost faith

Mr. Fisher.   20.

in its general, and he has on numerous occasions proved his weaknesses, only one thing can be done. He has very seldom been at Anzac. He lives at Imbros. The French call him the General who lives on an Island. The story may not be true, but the army believes that Hamilton left Suvla on August 21 remarking " Everything hangs in the balance, the Yeomanry are about to charge." Of course the army laughs at a general who leaves the battlefield when everything hangs in the balance.

    I could make this letter interminable, and I fear that I have only touched very incompletely on a few phases. What I want to say to you now very seriously is that the continuous and ghastly bungling over the Dardanelles enterprise was to be expected from such a General Staff as the British Army possesses, so far as I have seen it. The conceit and self-complacency of the red feather men are equalled only by their incapacity. Along the line of communications, and especially at Mudros, are countless high officers and conceited young cubs who are plainly only playing at war. What can you expect of men who have never worked seriously, who have lived for their appearance and for social distinction and selfsatisfaction, and who are now called on to conduct a gigantic war ? Kitchener has a terrible task in getting pure work out of these men, whose motives can never be pure, for they are unchangeably selfish. I want to say frankly that it is my opinion, and that without exception of Australian officers, that appointments to the General Staff are made from motives of friendship and social influence. Australians now loathe and detest any Englishmen wearing red. Without such a purification of motive as will bring youth and ability to the top, we cannot win. I could tell you

Mr. Fisher.   21.

of many scandals, but the instance that will best appeal to you is
that/the staff ship Aragon. She is a magnificent and luxurious South
American liner, anchored in Mudros harbour as a base for the Staff
of the Inspector-General of Communications. I can give you no idea
of how the Australians - and the new British officers too - loathe
the Aragon. Heaven knows what she is costing, but certainly the staff
lives in luxury. And nothing can exceed the rudeness of these
chocolate general staff soldiers to those returning from the front.
The ship's adjutant is the worst instance of rude and disgusting
snobbishness and incapacity I have come across. With others, plain
downright incapacity is the main characteristic. I must say this of
them also, that whereas at our 3rd Australian General Hospital on
shore we had 134 fever cases, including typhus, with only a few mosquito nets, and no ice, and few medical comforts, the Aragon staff
was wallowing in ice. Colonel Stawell - you know him as Melbourne's
leading consultant - and Sir Alex. M'Cormick are not sentimentalists.
But they really wept over the terrible hardships of the wounded, due
to the incapacity of the Aragon. One concrete case is that of 150
wounded men landed in dead of night, with no provision and no instructions, at the hospital beach, to make their way as best they could to
the hospital, which had no notice of their arrival. Fiaschi, de
Crespigny, Stawell and Kent Hughes will be able to tell you of the
absolutely shocking difficulties of this hospital in face of perpetual
snubbing and bungling of the Aragon staff. While I was at the hospital
a beautiful general and his staff rode in to make an inspection.
Despite their appearance as perfect specimens of the general staff,
I thought, we shall now get the ice from the Aragon on to the brows

Mr. Fisher.   22.

of our unfortunate men. But no ice appeared next day. The navy is very good, and sent some comforts and ice across, but for the three days before my visit this ice had gone astray before it reached the hospital.

I told you in my last letter of the necessity for canteen ships, and need not go into that now, but on the point of the general staff I must say that the work at the bases in Egypt struck me as on a par with that of the Aragon. Some day you will have to take up the case of Sir John Maxwell. He has a poor brain for his big position, and I assure you that our officers at Anzac have a poor opinion of the work of his lieutenant, General Spens [- a man broken on the continent, and therefore thought good enough to supervise the training of Australians] who is controlling our bases. The question you will have to fight out about Maxwell is this. After the last disturbance in the Whasa, when a very few of our men burnt some houses in which they had been drugged and diseased, he issued one of his famous lecturing orders, in which he referred to his regret that "even wilful murder" had been mentioned as one of the Australian crimes in Cairo. In this casual way did he blast the good name of our clean and vigorous army. I inquired as far as was possible, and could hear nothing of even a charge of wilful murder mentioned against any Australian. This order roused intense anger amongst our men. Perhaps we are too sensitive -. Our men were certainly too sensitive in their anger in the trenches when a notice was posted, I think in orders, describing how an unfortunate British Tommy had been shot at Helles at dawn for cowardice. It was almost amusing to hear our men resent this even remote connection with the Australian forces and a

FACSIMILE OF THE GALLIPOLI LETTER

PLATE 12   A view of the long wooden pier leading to Anzac Cove, taken on the last day of the occupation. An unidentified soldier is standing at the end of the jetty. *AWM Neg. No. A01868*

Mr. Fisher.   23.

veiled threat of such shooting. " Such things have nothing to do with us," they said.

Our men feel that their reputation is too sacred to leave in the hands of Maxwell, and they much resent the sudden change in the attitude of the general staff, which regarded them as criminals in Cairo, and now lavishly calls them heroes in Gallipoli.

You will think that all this is a sorry picture, but do not forget that the enemy has his troubles, and that we have certain signs that his morale is deteriorating. From what I saw of the Turk I am convinced that he is a brave and generous foe, and he is fighting now for dear home, with a feeling that he is winning, and that he is a better man than those opposed to him. The Turks by the way are as generous in their praise of our men as the British and French are. Certainly the Turks are positively afraid of our men, and one of their trenches - that opposite Quinn's Post - is such a place of fear, owing to the indomitable way in which our snipers and bomb-throwers have got their men down, that Turks will not go into it unless they are made corporals. So say our Intelligence Officers. I saw many strange and remarkable instances of the humanity and courage of the Turks. Certainly his trenches are better than anything we can do, and he makes them remarkably quickly.

One word more to-day. Do for Heaven's sake make every effort to secure the recall of Sir James Porter, the Englishman in charge of the medical services. Our doctors are without exception furious with him. He made a shocking muddle of the first arrangements for transport of wounded, as I wrote you. The case against him there was unanswerable. But he has been left in charge, and his muddling

Mr. Fisher.   24.

continues. He lives on a luxurious yacht in Mudros. Oh, no Australian has the heart to tell of the fearful wreckage of life due to this man's incompetency. That is not a wild statement. It is truth. Even now, the great bulk of the wounded are sent to Imbros before being passed on to hospitals elsewhere. This handling aggravates sickness and wounds, yet the Generals wonder why men sent away from the peninsula with slight sickness become worse and do not, as expected, return in a few weeks - do not return at all. Our Australian doctors have bearded Porter in his den, and talked open defiance to him, in the vain hope that he would insist on an inquiry, or lay a charge against them. We must make the best of the R.A.M.C., but we surely need not be burdened with Porter's sins. After having heard and seen something of the awful bungling of the wounded transport arrangements, one wonders how it is possible that the War Office should regard with complacency the prospect of leaving this man the very difficult work of getting sick and wounded from the peninsula during the winter. The only reason I can think of is that professional soldiers stick to each other through thick and thin.

      I hope I have not made the picture too gloomy. I have great faith still in the Englishman. And, as I have said, the enemy is having his own troubles too. But this unfortunate expedition has never been given a chance. It required large bodies of seasoned troops. It required a great leader. It required self-sacrifice on the part of the staff as well as that sacrifice so wonderfully and liberally made on the part of the soldiers. It has had none of these things. Its troops have been second class, because untried before their awful battles and privations of the peninsula. And behind it

THE GALLIPOLI LETTER

Mr. Fisher.   25.

all is a gross selfishness and complacency on the part of the staff.

Much more I could tell you, but my task is done, though I shall write again next mail - I hope with better news. This of course is a private letter, but you will show it to George Pearce and Hughes, so I shall say nothing more than the plain good-bye of a friend.

Sincerely yours,